ORDINARY PEOPLE, EXTRAORDINARY ACTIONS

ORDINARY PEOPLE, EXTRAORDINARY ACTIONS

Refuge Through Activism
at Ottawa's St. Joe's Parish

Stéfanie Morris, Karina Juma, Meredith Terretta,
and Patti Tamara Lenard

University of Ottawa Press
2022

University of Ottawa **Press**
Les **Presses** de l'Université d'Ottawa

The University of Ottawa Press (UOP) is proud to be the oldest of the francophone university presses in Canada and the oldest bilingual university publisher in North America. Since 1936, UOP has been enriching intellectual and cultural discourse by producing peer-reviewed and award-winning books in the humanities and social sciences, in French and in English.

www.press.uottawa.ca

Library and Archives Canada Cataloguing in Publication

Title: Ordinary people, extraordinary actions : refuge through activism at Ottawa's St. Joe's Parish / Stéfanie Morris, Karina Juma, Meredith Terretta and Patti Tamara Lenard.
Names: Morris, Stéfanie, author. | Juma, Karina, author. | Terretta, Meredith, author. | Lenard, Patti Tamara, 1975- author.
Series: Politics and public policy (University of Ottawa Press)
Description: Series statement: Politics and public policy | Includes bibliographical references.
Identifiers: Canadiana (print) 20210369698 | Canadiana (ebook) 20210369779 | ISBN 9780776629704 (hardcover) | ISBN 9780776629698 (softcover) | ISBN 9780776629711 (PDF) | ISBN 9780776629728 (EPUB)
Subjects: LCSH: St. Joseph's Parish (Ottawa, Ont.). Refugee Outreach Committee. | LCSH: Church work with refugees—Ontario—Ottawa. | LCSH: Refugees—Services for—Ontario—Ottawa. | LCSH: Syrians—Ontario—Ottawa.
Classification: LCC BV4466 .M67 2022 | DDC 261.8/3280971384—dc23

Legal Deposit: Second Quarter 2022
Library and Archives Canada

© Stéfanie Morris, Karina Juma, Meredith Terretta, and Patti Tamara Lenard 2022

The University of Ottawa Press gratefully acknowledges the support extended to its publishing list by the Government of Canada, the Canada Council for the Arts, the Ontario Arts Council, the Social Sciences and Humanities Research Council and the Canadian Federation for the Humanities and Social Sciences through the Awards to Scholarly Publications Program, and by the University of Ottawa.

ONTARIO ARTS COUNCIL
CONSEIL DES ARTS DE L'ONTARIO
an Ontario government agency
un organisme du gouvernement de l'Ontario

Canada Council Conseil des arts
for the Arts   du Canada

Canadä

u Ottawa

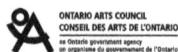

This digital watercolour artwork, by Evan Murtadha, was made in Procreate especially for this book. It depicts a whimsical scene in a style that is part Modernist and part Impressionist.

The picture depicts the emotional scene, described in the book, where members of St Joseph's Refugee Outreach Committee—in blue (the colour of their logo) welcomed refuge-seekers and other newcomers to their new, safe, home in Canada.

Ottawa—Canada's capital—is depicted as a watercolour skyline in the light of a beautiful sunrise.

Table of Contents

Abbreviations

BVOR	Blended Visa Office-Referred
CCR	Canadian Council for Refugees
CCI	Catholic Centre for Immigrants
CRR	Capital Rainbow Refuge
ECG	English Conversation Group
GAR	Government-Assisted Refugee
H&C	Humanitarian and compassionate grounds
IRB	Immigration and Refugee Board of Canada
IRPA	*Immigration and Refugee Protection Act*
JAS	Joint Assistance Sponsorship
LGBTQ+	Lesbian, gay, bisexual, transgender, queer or questioning, and other people of diverse sexual orientations and gender identity
OMI	The Oblates (Missionary Oblates of Mary Immaculate)
PRRA	Pre-Removal Risk Assessment
PSR	Privately Sponsored Refugee
PSRP	Private Sponsorship of Refugees Program
RAD	Refugee Appeal Division
ROC	St. Joseph's Parish Refugee Outreach Committee
RSCJ	Religious of the Sacred Heart of Jesus (Religieuses du Sacré-Cœur de Jésus)
RSTP	Refugee Sponsorship Training Program
SAH	Sponsorship Agreement Holder
UNHCR	United Nations High Commissioner for Refugees (also known as the United Nations' Refugee Agency)
UNRWA	United Nations Relief and Works Agency
WUSC	World University Service of Canada

Acknowledgements

A book of this type relies on the willingness of people to tell their stories, and we are grateful especially to the members of St. Joseph's Refugee Outreach Committee (ROC) for their openness in doing so. We are even more grateful for the opportunity to learn about, and share with our readers, the tremendous good they have done over many years.

This book would also never have been written without the meticulous records and notes kept over thirty years by dedicated members of St. Joseph's ROC. In particular, we are inspired by Louise Lalonde's foresight in maintaining a tradition of record-keeping. We will never think of meeting minutes as trivial again. Without them, meaningful details of the ROC's efforts and refuge-seekers' stories would have been lost.

To our interviewees: the time we spent learning from you was precious and we are so grateful that you welcomed us into your confidence. We hope that you will love this book. Many more volumes could have been written about St. Joe's Committee members and the lives of the newcomers they served.

To our reviewers: thank you for sharing your time during a global pandemic and finding the bandwidth to provide kind and constructive feedback.

We would also like to thank Evan Murtadha for her work on the beautiful cover image for this book; Madeleine Berry for formatting the manuscript to prepare it for publication; the friendly and encouraging staff at University of Ottawa Press for supporting the publication of this book; and the Social Sciences and Humanities Research Council for funding this project.

The events in this book and our research work took place primarily in Ottawa, which is the unceded and traditional territory of the Algonquin Anishinabe. We respect and honour their rights as traditional guardians of this beautiful land.

Timeline: 1990-2020

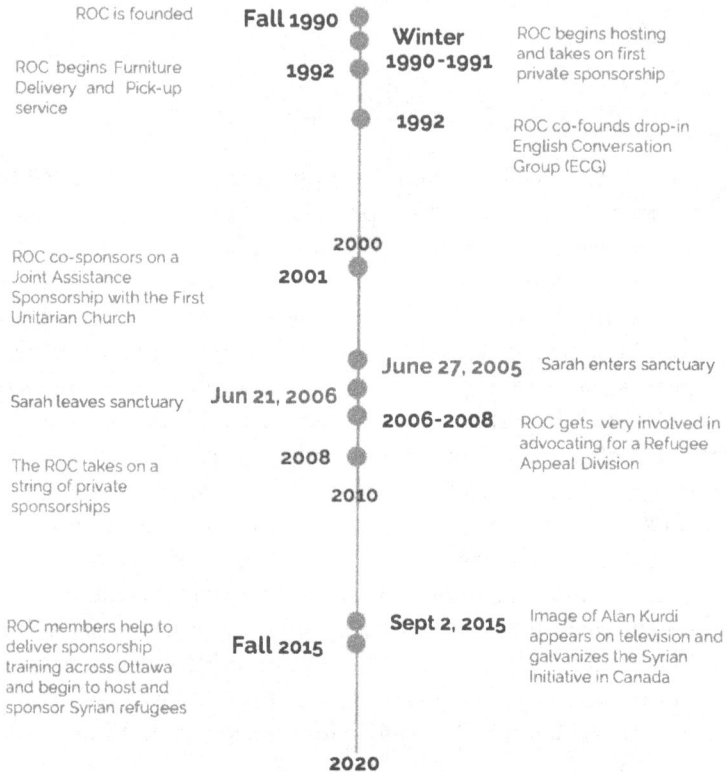

ROC is founded | **Fall 1990**

Winter 1990-1991 — ROC begins hosting and takes on first private sponsorship

ROC begins Furniture Delivery and Pick-up service | **1992**

1992 — ROC co-founds drop-in English Conversation Group (ECG)

2000

ROC co-sponsors on a Joint Assistance Sponsorship with the First Unitarian Church | **2001**

June 27, 2005 — Sarah enters sanctuary

Sarah leaves sanctuary | **Jun 21, 2006**

2006-2008 — ROC gets very involved in advocating for a Refugee Appeal Division

The ROC takes on a string of private sponsorships | **2008**

2010

ROC members help to deliver sponsorship training across Ottawa and begin to host and sponsor Syrian refugees | **Fall 2015**

Sept 2, 2015 — Image of Alan Kurdi appears on television and galvanizes the Syrian Initiative in Canada

2020

Introduction

L ush with greenery in the summer and frozen over in the winter, Ottawa is the seat of Canada's federal government. In a city where you can walk off the light rail train and cross paths with the prime minister, or picnic on the lawn of the Supreme Court, residents have long played a pivotal role in shaping Canadian policy and identity through their activism and advocacy. This influence has been especially significant in matters of immigration and refugee policy.

Canada's history has been deeply marred by discriminatory laws and policies. Since its colonial beginnings, Canada has evolved as a state to legislatively favour the settlement of predominantly white Christians (Walker 2008). Over the last century, Canada's acceptance of refugees fleeing persecution has been mixed. As Irving Abella and Harold Troper recount in *None Is Too Many: Canada and the Jews of Europe 1933–1948*, before and throughout World War II, Canada largely shut its doors to Jews who sought protection after fleeing Europe. In 1939, Canada's Mackenzie King government refused safe landing to 907 German Jews aboard the MS *St. Louis* on approach to Halifax Harbour, forcing them to return to Belgium. The decision sealed the fate of 254 people aboard who did not survive the Holocaust.

Despite the Canadian government's historical reluctance in accepting refuge-seekers, advocates from religious and community groups have long played an important role in pressing the government to adopt more liberal refugee policies. Groups such as the Canadian Christian Council for the Resettlement of Refugees (CCCRR), the Canadian Jewish Congress (CJC), and the Canadian Council of Churches (CCC) were at the forefront of lobbying the government after World War II to extend refugee programs, to allow them to sponsor non-relatives. They were ultimately successful. At least sixty thousand displaced people arrived in Canada between

April 1947 and March 1952 through an evolving, church-led private sponsorship program (Cameron 2020, 23). Private sponsorship allowed Canadian citizens and permanent residents to select or "name" refugees abroad whom these sponsors would commit to fund and support during their first year of resettlement in Canada. Private sponsors helped make arrangements for refugees' accommodations, health care, education, language and job training, and other services. In 1956–1957, these same groups advocated for and facilitated the resettlement of 37,565 Hungarian refugees (2020, 27).

Such concessions were not easily won. Faith communities contested the government over the eligibility of certain refuge-seekers, their access to welfare after arriving in Canada, and whether they should be selected to meet labour demands or for humanitarian reasons (Cameron 2021). Private sponsorship was also extremely vulnerable; it remained a policy that the federal government could terminate at will. Yet, due to the determination and pressure of faith communities and coalitions, the 1978 *Immigration Act* formally included private sponsorship in law for the first time.[1]

The Act's provisions were tested immediately. From 1975 to 1980, an estimated 1.4 million Southeast Asian refugees fled their homelands in the aftermath of the Vietnam War (Carrière 2016). Some fled overland, but as many as three hundred thousand departed by sea. In early 1979, newspapers and television screens transmitted images of the refuge-seekers whom the Canadian public came to know as "the Boat People."

In Ottawa, residents watching from their living rooms were shocked by the images they saw on their televisions that year. They watched people fleeing their homes, crowding in ports and camps, loading onto leaking, sinking boats, and being refused landing in neighbouring nations. Among the viewers was newly elected Ottawa Mayor Marion Dewar, who saw these images while on a weekend trip with her husband and friends in the Laurentians (Gorham 2016). Compelled to do *something*, Mayor Dewar, a devoted Catholic, convened a meeting upon returning to work on June 27, 1979. She invited

---

1   Section 115(I)(k.I) of the *Immigration Act 1978* states that the Governor in Council can make any regulations "where a person or organization seeks to facilitate the admission or arrival in Canada of a Convention refugee … establishing the requirements to be met by any such person or organization including the provision of an undertaking to assist any such Convention refugee, person or immigrant in becoming successfully established in Canada.…"

trusted advisors, faith leaders in her community, and the federal Minister of Immigration, Ron Atkey. The Minister was unable to attend and sent a senior official in his stead. Up to this point, the federal government had resettled a modest nine thousand Southeast Asian refugees between 1975 and 1978 (Molloy et al. 2017, 8). When Mayor Dewar pressed the Minister's senior official to understand what more could be done, the official responded by saying that the Canadian government had already funded and supported the resettlement of four thousand of their eight thousand Southeast Asian refugee quota. Exasperated by the government's apparent lack of urgency, Mayor Dewar reportedly responded on behalf of her city, "Fine. We'll take the other four thousand" (Gorham 2016).

Mayor Dewar stuck to her word and launched Project 4000 to support individuals who wished to privately sponsor refugees from Southeast Asia. By July 4, the Ottawa City Council had voted to support the mayor's project and budgeted twenty-five thousand dollars to do so. Much more community support was needed though. The provisions in the 1978 *Immigration Act* made it possible for religious or voluntary organizations to sign agreements with the federal government and commit to support a refugee's resettlement (Molloy et al. 2017). Additionally, another significant provision in the Act made it possible for groups of five or more citizens or permanent residents to sponsor a refugee if they had the capacity to assume full responsibility, including financial, for their reception and settlement.

To reach the public, Mayor Dewar convinced the editors of both the *Ottawa Citizen* and the *Ottawa Journal* of the importance of quickly resettling Southeast Asian refugees. Both editors agreed to enthusiastically promote it. On July 4, the *Ottawa Journal* wrote an editorial calling it a "brave initiative" and "the most humanitarian gesture this community has demonstrated in many years" (Gorham 2016). The *Ottawa Citizen* even printed a sponsorship form on its front page; anyone who wanted to participate in sponsoring a refuge-seeker could submit the form to the newspaper, whose staff then divided volunteers into sponsorship groups of thirty or so households in the same neighbourhood (Powell 2014).

On July 12, the city held a public rally at Lansdowne Park, which, incredibly, was attended by around three thousand people seeking to get involved. Faith-based organizations and communities were at the forefront of all planning due to their influence and evolving role in matters of settlement in the community. Catholic Archbishop Plourde,

Anglican Bishop William Robinson, and Rabbi Don Gerber of the new Jewish Reform congregation, Temple Israel, were among the speakers at the event.

Members of the public responded with overwhelming support. The government soon found itself trying to keep pace with a surge of sponsorship commitments from across the country. Private sponsorship quickly became a household term. In response to increasing public support and pressure, the newly elected federal government, under Prime Minister Joe Clark's leadership, agreed to increase the quota of refugees that Canada was willing to resettle from eight thousand to fifty thousand. The government went on to sign major private sponsorship agreements with forty faith-based organizations also seeking to facilitate resettlement (Cameron 2021, 158).

In the end, nearly sixty thousand Southeast Asian refugees, of which approximately thirty-four thousand were privately sponsored, found safety in Canada between 1979 and 1982. Nearly seven thousand sponsoring groups participated across Canada (Cameron 2020, 33).

When Ottawa's Project 4000 wrapped up in 1980, roughly two thousand refugees had been resettled in Ottawa through private sponsorship and 1,600 under the federal government's initiative. Per capita, Ottawa likely took in more Southeast Asian refugees than any other Canadian community. Mayor Dewar has been widely praised for her part in starting a movement. In later years, when pressed about her role in responding to the crisis in Southeast Asia, Mayor Dewar described herself as ordinary (Gorham 2016). Certainly, she deserves commendation for using her power and moral authority as a leader in her community to challenge the public and the government to greater action. Yet her comment serves as a reminder that her intervention was only part of the story. Thousands of people in Canada have participated in similar ways, using whatever influence they have had at their disposal then and in years since, to ensure welcome and protection to refuge-seekers. This book aims to tell the stories of others, like Mayor Dewar, who have done just this.

* * *

At the time of writing, in 2021, if we had asked Canadians what they know about Canada's support for refuge-seekers, they would probably recall the harrowing image of three-year-old Syrian Alan Kurdi's body lying lifeless on a Turkish shore on September 2, 2015.

The widely circulated image of the boy, whose aunt Tima Kurdi resided in Canada (Kurdi 2018), spurred Liberal Party leader Justin Trudeau's election pledge to resettle twenty-five thousand refugees by the end of 2015. In the months following the federal election, the new Trudeau government only achieved this target with the help of the public. As in the late 1970s, Canadian residents—Syrian Canadians, neighbours, friends, faith communities, advocacy groups, and settlement organizations—again mobilized to create and fund private sponsorship groups; to gather donations of winter jackets, backpacks, furniture, and more; and to volunteer in other ways to support settlement organizations.

The events surrounding the initiative to resettle Syrians have been the subject of much research in recent years (Labman and Cameron 2020; Hamilton, Veronis, and Walton-Roberts 2020; Reynolds and Clark-Kazak 2019; Canadian Ethnic Studies 2018). This interest stems, in large part, from the unique role of private individuals who volunteer for and sponsor Canada's settlement efforts. In Canada, tens of thousands of volunteers have given their time, for no pay and often outside of their regular work hours, even in addition to other volunteer work, to support the reception and settlement of refuge-seekers (Wilson 2012; Verba, Lehman Schlozman, and Brady 1995; Fraser Institute 2017; Gouthro 2010).

Historically, Canada's settlement sector—meaning all formal and informal organizations, institutions, and services intended for newcomers, immigrants, and refuge-seekers—has largely grown through the persistent efforts of faith communities and faith-based organizations. In Ottawa, before sponsorship became a rallying point, one of the very first services for newcomers and immigrants was established by the Catholic Archdiocese in 1953: a small drop-in centre run by Sister Thérèse Dallaire, of the Filles de la Sagesse, at the old registry office on Nicholas Street (OCISO 2019). Sister Dallaire also coordinated Ottawa's Interfaith Committee on Immigrants, an advocacy group that included representatives from all the major churches in the city.

Sister Dallaire's efforts and those of many others in the community led to the formal establishment of the Catholic Centre for Immigrants (CCI) in 1976 (though at that time it was known as the Catholic Immigration Centre). CCI began in a modest fashion with an office in the Archdiocesan Centre and a board of directors to provide guidance on policy. They aimed to receive and welcome immigrants, offer them information and referral advice, and advocate on their behalf when necessary (Rapley 2004). Small as it was, CCI relied on a dedicated base of volunteers, primarily from within the Catholic community. By 1979, as the City of Ottawa rolled out Project 4000, CCI's role grew quickly, as they received funding to help coordinate sponsorships and settlement services for the wave of newly resettled refugees. By the 1980s, CCI became an independent, community-based organization, allowing it to access more funding from the government while maintaining its traditionally Catholic volunteer support.

This brief history highlights the foundational role played by faith-based organizations and communities in the development of Canada's willingness and ability to provide protection for refuge-seekers. Yet studies show that religious commitment among Canadians is declining (Wilkins-Laflamme 2015). Evidence also suggests that Canada's most active volunteers are among the healthy elderly, and Canada's volunteer population is generally aging (Vézina and Crompton 2012; Turcotte 2015). These societal changes are troubling factors with respect to refugee sponsorship and other settlement programs. The structure of current refugee programs assumes that faith communities will be major players and motivates them to continue filling a significant role (Chapman 2014; McKinlay 2008; Quan 2015). If fewer Canadians relate to faith communities, and volunteerism in general is declining as volunteers age, then refugee advocates must focus explicitly on identifying and amplifying the conditions that enable volunteers to support refuge-seekers.

It is urgent that refugee advocates come to a better understanding of why "ordinary people" choose to dedicate their time to emotionally and materially supporting refugees in Canada. What motivates them to do this work, both in times of perceived refugee crises and over time? Considering volunteers' vital role in settlement, what causes them to abandon this activism? What do they require— from the government, from activist networks, from settlement organizations, and from the public at large—to continue doing their work? How do Canadian policies encourage or discourage volunteers working to welcome refuge-seekers?

The purpose of this book is to answer some of these questions. In particular, we do so by telling the stories of how one faith community in Ottawa—St. Joseph's Parish—has participated in sponsorship and settlement for over thirty years.

* * *

St. Joseph's Parish is a Catholic parish located in the Sandy Hill neighbourhood of downtown Ottawa. It was founded by the Missionary Oblates of Mary Immaculate (hereafter referred to as the Oblates), the religious order that also founded what is now the University of Ottawa (Byrne 2007). The Oblates were formed in 1816 in France by Eugène de Mazenod, a bishop in Marseille who petitioned the Pope to create a special order. He wanted to form a community of priests dedicated to serving the poor and those most marginalized in the Church, who would live among the people and speak their languages. The order spread and six Oblate priests came to Canada in 1841, two of whom settled in the Ottawa area in 1844 (Byrne 2007, 3).

The Oblates played a significant role in Canadian settler colonialism. In recent years, Canadian settlers have begun to come to terms with the legacy of Indian Residential Schools, a majority of which were founded and run by the Oblates in the nineteenth century. The residential school system operated officially from the 1880s and into the closing decades of the twentieth century and aimed to assimilate Indigenous children by separating them from their homes, families, communities, cultures, and languages. Children in these schools experienced abuse of all kinds. The residential school system continues to have a significant impact on Indigenous communities to this day (TRC 2016).

In 1991, the Oblates made a formal apology to the First Nations of Canada for their role in the "cultural, ethnic, linguistic, and religious imperialism" that structured Canadian society, in particular the relationship between settlers and Indigenous peoples, as well as for their part in establishing and maintaining the residential schools that violated familial bonds and subjected Indigenous children to "physical and sexual abuse that occurred in those schools" (OMI 1991). As an Oblate Parish, St. Joseph's also recognizes the Oblates' significant role in this aspect of Canada's settler colonialism. As we write this book, the parish community has organized masses and prayer sessions centering the news of the discovery of the unmarked graves of 215 children at Tk'emlúps te Secwépemc, on the grounds of the former Oblate-run Kamloops Residential School (St. Joseph's Parish 2021). St. Joseph's parishioners are on a path to reconciliation to acknowledge the truth about parish history in settler colonialism and the structural racism it engendered.

In line with these efforts, St. Joseph's Parish, affectionately known as St. Joe's, has gained a reputation for its emphasis on social justice and for doing things a little differently. Over the years, it has drawn in Catholics looking for a faith community to challenge them to action. Historically, St. Joe's leaders have evolved "towards a more universal church..." as one long-time parishioner explained. Parishioners remember recurring homilies about serving the poor, human rights, and social justice.

In step with this commitment to social justice, St. Joe's has long managed two important public-serving ministries in downtown Ottawa: the Supper Table and the Women's Centre. Both are still active to this day. The Supper Table, established in 1978, provides food for those in need by serving a hot supper to hundreds every weekday. The Women's Centre, established in 1984, is a safe daytime meeting place for women seeking different forms of support in the community. The Women's Centre also offers a wide range of social and educational programming.

This book focuses particularly on the development of a third ministry at St. Joe's, beginning in 1990, dedicated to assisting refuge-seekers in the community.[2] A small group of passionate parishioners formed the Parish's Refugee Outreach Committee, now most often referred to as the "ROC" (pronounced like "rock"). Thirty years later, the ROC is still active and its members are still advocating for the rights of refuge-seekers in the heart of Canada's capital. In these thirty years, more than 125 ROC members have hosted and sponsored over two hundred refuge-seekers and immigrants in their community. Many more were supported through other services such as the ROC's Furniture Pick-up and Delivery Service and an ecumenical English Conversation Group.

The stories in this book rely on oral accounts and centre the voices of ROC members and the refuge-seekers they welcomed. They also draw on meticulous ROC records, kept by Louise Lalonde and many others since 1990, comprised of minutes from nearly every

2   This book is the product of research undertaken as part of a study funded by the Social Sciences and Humanities Research Council (SSHRC) entitled "Local Activism, Global Impact: A Case-Study of St. Joseph's Parish Refugee Outreach Committee." The project was co-directed by Professors Patti Tamara Lenard (Graduate School of Public and International Affairs) and Meredith Terretta (Department of History). Stéfanie Morris and Karina Juma were research assistants on the project.

Committee meeting since its inception; a full record of parish news-letters which detail its everyday challenges; communications among members as key decisions were made; relevant newspaper clippings and media reports; fundraising brochures; and miscellaneous other archival material.

In the fall of 2019, we began speaking with past and present ROC members. Louise Lalonde, Pierre Gauthier, Greg Humbert, Irene Kellow, Margie Cain, Michael McBane, Rosemary Williams, Robyne Warren, John Weir, Michèle Gascon, Mary Murphy, Radamis Zaky, Kevin Doyle, Jessica Silva, Deborah Dorner, and Joe Gunn have all contributed their accounts. We also spoke with parishioners and community members who were either in close contact with the ROC over the years or who also played a role in similar groups across the country, including Laura Guillemette (from Paroisse Sacré-Coeur), Marsha Wilson (St. Joseph's Women's Centre), Norma McCord (CCI and the United Church of Canada Refugee Advisory Group), Terry Byrne (St. Joseph's Parish historian), Shelly Lawrence (Religious of the Sacred Heart), Don Smith (Anglican Diocese of Ottawa), Louisa Taylor (Refugee 613), Michael Bossin (Community Legal Services of Ottawa), Peter Showler (former chair of the Immigration and Refugee Board), Christina Clark-Kazak (Associate Professor at the University of Ottawa), Rabbi Liz Bolton (Ottawa's Reconstructionist Community), and Kailee Brennan (Safe Harbour, Pictou County). These conversations were typically semi-structured in order to allow interviewees to direct the narrative of their accounts. Conversations were held in homes, coffee shops, in St. Joseph's, and later, because of the COVID-19 pandemic, over video conference or by phone call.

We also spoke with six past refuge-seekers who received support from the ROC. In order to protect their privacy, their names and as many identifying details as possible have been omitted from the book and replaced with pseudonyms (chosen by the individuals themselves where possible). Their perspectives have been vital to understanding the nature of the relationships built over thirty years between ROC members and those they welcomed. Many of the former refuge-seekers welcomed by the ROC are now Canadian citizens. Some have in turn helped to bring their own family members to Canada or have volunteered to assist the ROC in welcoming other newcomers. Through this book, we especially hope to demonstrate how reciprocal and enriching such relationships were and can be under the right circumstances. From birthdays to graduations to exploring their city, ROC members report that they have gained as much if not more than they have given from the new Canadians they welcomed.

Throughout the book we incorporate many direct quotations and summarize first-hand narratives taken from the archives and our interviews[3] in order to capture, as much as possible, events as they appeared from the perspectives of those who lived these experiences and can tell the stories best. Unfortunately, we were not able to interview all the people involved in this work. The number of people who have participated in the ROC over the years is vast and their stories and perspectives could fill libraries. To ensure that the stories are representative of as many ROC members as possible, past and present ROC members—including Louise Lalonde, Pierre Gauthier, Irene Kellow, Margie Cain, John Weir, Radamis Zaky, and Dan Dorner—have reviewed an early draft of the book prior to its publication.

In this book, we frequently employ the term "refuge-seekers" to refer to resettled refugees and asylum seekers in order to challenge the notion of "refugee" as an enduring identity. Instead, we, like ROC members, understand the process of *seeking refuge* as an action that someone undertakes due to temporary life circumstances. However, at times we do employ the term refugee to distinguish between the different streams of refuge-seeking, such as, for example, asylum seekers/refugee claimants and resettled refugees. The ROC also assisted a (smaller) number of persons who immigrated to Canada for reasons other than to seek protection. We use the term immigrant in some accounts, both to refer to those who arrived through immigration rather than refugee programs and to refer to those who migrated to Canada more broadly when necessary.

We use the term "faith-based organization" to refer to formal, institutionalized organizations of a spiritual though not necessarily religious nature, whether an organization like St. Joe's Parish or a large advocacy group like the Canadian Council of Churches. In contrast, we refer to faith communities when writing more broadly about individuals affiliated with faith-based organizations or traditions.

---

3   When directly quoted material is presented in this book without another source being documented, readers can assume the material is from one of our interviews. Material taken from the ROC records will be cited as ROC Archives, along with the year the document is from.

The following chapters will recount the history of ROC's thirty years of service in the Ottawa community. The ROC's stories demonstrate the minute and massive influence of volunteers on programs and policy in Canada's settlement sector, whether as sponsors or hosts to resettled refugees, or as advocates for asylum seekers and immigrants.

We begin in Chapter 1, "Early Activism at St. Joes' Refugee Outreach Committee," with the ROC's first fifteen years (approximately 1990–2005), explaining the reasons for the ROC's inception and the motivations of its early members. We examine the institutional structure that amplified the ROC's activism and support for refuge-seekers and immigrants through hosting, sponsorship, and other programs. We then share perspectives on the settlement experience and the value of community organizations as explained by people the ROC served over the years. We connect these themes to the broader literature concerning the value of community participation in newcomer settlement and integration (Kaida, Hou, and Stick 2020; Woo and Stueck 2015).

In Chapter 2, "Advocacy through Sanctuary," and Chapter 3, "Post-Sanctuary Advocacy," we share stories of the ROC's sustained efforts for refugee claimants, beginning with their role in providing sanctuary to a woman we refer to as Sarah from 2005 to 2006 and then through their efforts to legislate for a Refugee Appeal Division (RAD). We contextualize the ROC's efforts within Canada's broader sanctuary movement and conversations about civil disobedience (Okafor 2020; Lippert 2005b).

In Chapter 4, "Decline and Resurgence: The Syrian Initiative," we tell the story of the years when the ROC's activity slowed and how the Trudeau government's decision in 2015 to resettle twenty-five thousand Syrian refugees helped re-energize resettlement volunteerism within the ROC, in Ottawa, and across Canada. Here we look at the ROC's participation in a number of Syrian sponsorships, hosting programs, and fundraisers, as well as their participation with a vast coalition of community advocates in the delivery of sponsorship training workshops around Ottawa. In their interactions with official programs for resettlement in recent years, the ROC has both supported and challenged the government's pathways and quotas for refugee admission.

Finally, in Chapter 5, "Longevity," we consider broader challenges that affect volunteer participation in private sponsorship and settlement. We also look at demographic changes in St. Joe's community and more broadly in Canada to discuss how shifts in religious practice and volunteerism in Canada as a whole affect the settlement sector. As we conclude, we identify how these societal changes challenge current assumptions about refugee sponsorship and other settlement programs, and we recommend ways to strengthen policies and programs to support volunteer retention and engagement.

* * *

The ROC is only one of thousands of groups across the country who work to welcome refuge-seekers in Canada. Without these groups, Canada would resettle and support far fewer refuge-seekers each year. Additionally, comparative data suggests that refuge-seekers who have community support, especially through private sponsorship, have better and quicker integration outcomes than those who do not (Bond and Kwadrans 2019, 87). If Canada hopes to continue supporting refuge-seekers in the long term—or to resettle them quickly in times of crisis, as they have promised to do with thousands of Afghans as we finalize this book (Keung 2021)—it is vital to understand what motivates people to do the challenging volunteer work of settlement and advocacy in both the short and long term.

In a 2018 visit to Canada, United Nations High Commissioner for Refugees Filippo Grandi said, "This is what I love about [Canada]: that civil society, *ordinary people*, NGOs, charitable organizations are very committed to helping people that come from abroad in search of safety, protection, and better lives" (UNHCR 2018; emphasis added). This book seeks to honour the activist spirit of the ordinary, extraordinary people—volunteers and refuge-seekers alike—across Canada who have played such an important role in refugee resettlement. St. Joe's ROC certainly had some unique opportunities to advocate on behalf of refuge-seekers due to their proximity to Parliament and their position in their community. However, many of their actions are relatable and feasible for any person or group who seeks to do similar work across Canada, including volunteering in settlement programs, sponsoring, speaking to political representatives, and maybe even providing sanctuary.

Such actions may even be possible beyond Canada. Indeed, in an attempt to mobilize ordinary people around the world to offer protection and support to refuge-seekers, the United Nations High

Commissioner for Refugees (UNHCR) has partnered with the Canadian government, the Open Society Foundations, the Giustra Foundation, and the University of Ottawa to encourage other communities in other countries to adopt contextually appropriate community sponsorship models. This partnership, called the Global Refugee Sponsorship Initiative (GRSI), works with countries to identify openings for private sponsorship and to support private individuals as they learn ways of supporting newly arrived refuge-seekers in their communities (IRCC 2020a; GRSI n.d.). In recent years, more than a dozen countries have explored the possibility of implementing such a program; pilot community sponsorship models have been implemented in the United Kingdom, Ireland, Spain, New Zealand, and Argentina (Bond and Kwadrans 2019; Manzanedo 2019; GRSI 2019). In February 2021, President Biden signed an Executive Order providing for the establishment of a private sponsorship program in the United States (Bier 2021).

The number of displaced people globally is at unprecedented levels, and border closures justified by combating the spread of the COVID-19 virus and its variants have made finding safety even more difficult for the world's most vulnerable people. As of June 2020, over thirty million refuge-seekers are displaced across international borders, and another nearly fifty million are internally displaced (UNHCR 2020). Correspondingly, the need to find innovative ways to support asylum seekers and refugees is greater than ever.

It is our hope that the extraordinary but everyday activism recounted in this history of St. Joe's ROC will serve as an inspiration for people and communities—young and old, secular and faith-oriented—across Canada and beyond as we collectively strive to strengthen our capacity to uphold asylum as a life-saving protection for those who need it.

Through this book, we wish to show how seemingly small decisions and actions have led to significant changes in policies and in people's lives—and how they can do so again in the future. This study of the ROC's thirty-year history enhances our understanding of what engages, motivates, and sustains community participation in settlement in the long term.

CHAPTER 1

Early Activism at St. Joe's Refugee Outreach Committee

S t. Joe's Refugee Outreach Committee (ROC) came to life in 1990, as
the world shook with events that still cast their shadow over the
present day. While the fall of the Berlin Wall marked the end of the
Cold War, other wars generated over eighteen million refugees—from
Angola, Afghanistan, Cambodia, El Salvador, the former Yugoslavia,
and beyond.

The ROC's foundation in 1990 was preceded by two important
events. In 1984, the federal government began piloting "host" programs
in a number of major cities across Canada. The goal of this program
was to match Canadian citizens with newly arrived Government-
Assisted Refugees (GARs). Unlike Privately Sponsored Refugees (PSRs),
who receive financial and emotional settlement support from sponsors
(usually faith-based organizations or community groups), GARs are
given income support by the federal government and matched with
settlement organizations that give them settlement support during the
first few months after arrival. The host programs that began to be developed—by the government and settlement organizations—in the eighties
were intended to allow GARs to receive the same emotional and informal community support that many PSRs had been receiving for years
through their sponsors. It was expected that host groups would help
refugees find permanent accommodations more quickly, help them
learn English or French, provide them with furniture and clothing, and
assist them in seeking employment (IRCC 2011; Refuge 1986).

By 1986, the government had implemented the host program in eleven of Canada's major cities. Though Ottawa was not among these, in 1987, a student studying social services at l'Université de Québec en Outaouais approached Ottawa's Catholic Centre for Immigrants (CCI) and offered to help them establish a short-term host program of sorts. The CCI was happy to accept the student's proposal when she offered to run it as part of her practicum. The program, a one-time year-long project, was called Bridge of Friendship, and the student set to work asking Catholic parishes in town to advertise for volunteers using their weekly parish bulletins.

The second event that laid the groundwork for the ROC's foundation was the arrival of a new parishioner at St. Joe's named Louise Lalonde. Louise was, and is still, a member of a Secular Institute, meaning that as a lay person, she pronounces vows of poverty, chastity and obedience and strives to live the mission of the laity as expressed in the Vatican II "Apostolate of the Laity," that is, to work at the transformation of the world from the inside, "like leaven in dough." She had recently returned from three years of service in Portugal, during which she had experienced first-hand the "alienation," as she put it, of being a newcomer. She had promised herself that upon her return to Canada, she would work with newcomers in her community.

Louise saw the CCI's Bridge of Friendship announcement in St. Joe's Parish bulletin and immediately volunteered. In the fall of 1987, she joined approximately fifteen volunteers at the first Bridge of Friendship meeting and became one of CCI's hosts. She was matched with a newcomer family of five that had just arrived from El Salvador— parents, two boys, and a girl. Louise recalls, "Much as I wanted to host, I felt a lot of anxiety about meeting the family. What did they expect from me? Did they know what a host's role was? Did they really want a host or were they too polite to refuse the offer?"

Her concerns were soon put to rest. With her limited Spanish— which she had learned in university eleven years earlier—Louise sent the family a letter introducing herself as their host and proposing a date and time for her first visit. They agreed to welcome her and on the appointed day, she arrived at their home with little gifts for the children. Using her broken Spanish, the children's English acquired in school, and hand gestures, they learned basic things about each other, and by the time the evening was over, Louise had overcome her apprehensions. They parted as friends and Louise promised to return weekly.

When Louise arrived for her second visit, she found Salvadoran friends of the family, a mother, who spoke English, and a six-year-old son from the same building, present as well and eager to be included in whatever it was that hosting had to offer. A few visits later, a single young man, also a tenant and friend of the daughter, began joining them too. Louise remembers: "While they appreciated my support during their process of integration into Canadian society, I was enriched by their culture and their example of generous hospitality."

Three months after the Bridge of Friendship program was established, the student coordinating the program left for personal reasons and was not replaced. By the end of the year, Louise was the only active host left. The host program was discontinued. CCI recognized Louise's desire to continue supporting refuge-seekers and newcomers and nominated her to their board of directors.

By 1990, CCI was able to obtain government funding to hire a part-time coordinator to renew and manage their host program. That same year, Ottawa's Catholic Archbishop Marcel Gervais called on CCI to launch a diocesan project for the private sponsorship of fifty Salvadoran refugees and to help support fifty more GARs, a project which required a hundred and fifty thousand dollars in funds to be raised through parish donations. All these factors were fertile ground for the foundation of St. Joe's ROC.

Spurred by these positive developments and her own recent experiences with refuge-seekers, Louise attended a symposium on immigrant and refugee issues sponsored by the Catholic Archdiocese of Ottawa-Cornwall and organized by CCI on April 27 and 28, 1990. She invited two fellow parishioners, Luc Young Chen Yin and Theresa Olsheskie, to join her. Surrounded by over a hundred Catholics and partners from fifty parishes and lay organizations, they listened as Archbishop Marcel Gervais shared the words of Pope John Paul II urging Christians to "seek to help [their] brother and sister refugees in every possible way" (John Paul II 1990). Archbishop Gervais urged each parish to establish a refugee committee focused on sponsoring and hosting refugees, helping them to integrate into Canadian society, and on sensitizing local communities to refugee issues.

Moved to action by this message, in May 1990, the three parishioners, Louise, Luc, and Theresa, returned to St. Joe's Parish and met with Gerry Morris, member of the Oblates and pastor of St. Joe's Parish, to discuss the formation of a refugee committee. His response was positive and enthusiastic. However, they all agreed that the predominantly white parish was not yet sufficiently informed or attuned to refugee issues to begin recruiting members to a new committee. They decided to spend the next few months sensitizing the community to the contemporary conflicts and challenges facing refuge-seekers around the world. The trio spent the summer crafting short messages, drawn from United Nations High Commissioner for Refugees (UNHCR) material, which were shared in the Parish's weekly bulletin.

In the fall, the trio prepared to recruit members at the Marketplace of Possibilities, St. Joe's fall volunteer festival. Feeling that a lot of the resistance Canadians had toward "refugees" arose because few had ever had the opportunity to meet any or listen to their experiences, the three parishioners chose to invite past refuge-seekers to share their stories at the Marketplace. After a few phone calls, they had three volunteers: a young Palestinian who had previously been a member of the Parish; a South Sudanese father of three, also a former parishioner; and an Anglican Ugandan woman who was studying at Saint Paul University.

In October on the day of the Marketplace, visitors were invited to draw a card from a deck relating to pre-selected questions they could pose to the guest speakers about their experiences as refuge-seekers. CCI also lent the Parish a poster display which illustrated different ways in which parishioners could get involved with refuge-seekers in Ottawa. The trio worried that the day's rainy weather would keep people away, but the booth drew a great number of parishioners and was the centre of enthusiastic conversation throughout the evening. By the end of the day, they had recruited twenty-two volunteers from a variety of backgrounds with various professional and personal talents—including a school counsellor, a seminarian, two lawyers, several public servants, a set of young parents, and a handful of retirees. To their excitement, this group also included a number of Spanish speakers and people who had previously worked abroad.

A few days later, on October 6, 1990, the ROC held its first meeting. Committee members discussed many questions: Where should meetings be held? How often? How would committee members be recruited and selected? Who would lead? What would be the ROC's mission? Some of the answers came easily enough: They agreed to meet monthly on the third Thursday of every month at 7:00 p.m. in the upstairs room of the rectory. They also decided they would select a chairperson, a secretary, and a treasurer annually. The chairperson would assure goals were met, facilitate decision-making, and represent the ROC at parish or community meetings. The secretary would prepare and maintain a record of minutes and agendas, ensuring their preservation over the years. The treasurer was to monitor the financial records and holdings of the ROC and deliver financial reports annually. Finally, decisions, whether on appointments or activities, were to be reached by consensus and vote.

Though the ROC held off on selecting its leadership for a few months as they defined their role, in their meeting of January 1991, they selected Louise, their founder and the most experienced member of the group, as their chair. Phillip Powell was selected to be both secretary and treasurer for the year.

That month, in an email to the ROC members, Louise wrote, "We have many reasons to be concerned about the state of our world and can be left feeling helpless. We can make a difference, though, by being the best we can be wherever we are and, hopefully, our work with refugees will make a difference in the community this year."

In time, Louise's hopes, along with those of all the early members, were solidified into a permanent mission statement that still serves the ROC today:

> We, the Refugee Outreach Committee,
> remembering St. Joseph's experience as a refugee (Matthew 2: 13–18)
> are called to welcome newcomers to our midst:
> to reach out to them, responding to their needs
> by offering support and friendship.
>
> We are called to promote in our community
> a spirit of openness and welcoming,
> an understanding and celebration of our differences
> and an awareness of refugee issues in the world.

* * *

"Any committee is only as good as the most knowledgeable, determined, and vigorous person on it," Lady Bird Johnson once wrote (Johnson 1970). Yet, in its early days, the ROC drew in a number of such people who dedicated their evenings, weekends, holidays, retirements, and hearts to carving out space for refuge-seekers and immigrants in religious and secular parts of their community.

The ROC's early members joined for a variety of reasons, some, because of their own experiences as immigrants. Louise Lalonde initiated the foundation of the ROC because of a promise she had made to herself while in Portugal that one day she would use her experience of isolation to help others in similar situations. Other ROC members had immigrated to Canada. Luc Young Chen Yin, a founding member originally from Rodrigues Island, Mauritius, had come to Canada as a seminarian studying at Saint Paul University. Irene Kellow joined in 1993, soon after moving to Ottawa from Toronto. She had come to Canada as an immigrant from the United Kingdom in the 1950s. Both she and her husband (an immigrant from Hong Kong) felt an affinity with newcomers to Canada who were trying to fit in.

Yet Irene and many other ROC members also joined because of their deep commitment to social justice. In Peterborough, Irene had volunteered with her prior parish's refugee committee, privately sponsoring families from Vietnam and Poland. In Toronto, she was active in her parish's Development and Peace branch. When she discovered that St. Joe's had a group dedicated to refugees, it felt like a natural progression. Marg Quinn, who joined in 1993, was another passionate advocate for social justice and played a prominent role on the ROC for thirteen years. Before moving from Toronto to Ottawa to take care of her aging parents, she had worked for a time at the Niagara border with refugees coming from El Salvador. Though she passed away in 2011, one member remembers her as their "guiding light," evoking her quiet personality and exemplary commitment. Her peers remember her as having contributed a great deal of wisdom and sensitivity to the ROC, in particular by drawing their attention to the needs of underserved refugee claimants and those experiencing homelessness.

Rosemary Williams joined the ROC in 1992. She remembers her parents teaching her the importance of sharing wealth and promoting the dignity of the poor. After working for Oxfam International in Oxford (UK) for a time, Rosemary moved to Newfoundland. There she helped establish her community's first Oxfam committee and ran in social justice circles of St. John's Archdiocese. When she and her husband decided to move to Ottawa in 1992, a friend she had known previously in Strasbourg, France, who shared her social justice–oriented Christian leaning told her, "There's only one parish for you," and directed her to St. Joe's, where she quickly joined the ROC.

Some ROC members joined almost by happenstance, others by invitation, but all soon became essential to the work. Margo Gauthier began attending St. Joe's in the spring of 1992, when she met Louise, who invited her to attend a committee meeting. Soon she enlisted her husband, Pierre Gauthier, as well. They had long been motivated by a desire to serve in their community. Margo had previously taught as a nurse at the University of Ottawa until she joined her husband to work in the auto industry. Pierre loved the politics of high investment and they continued to work in this sector for twenty years. In their fifties, they realized that they were in a position to retire early and stop their pursuit "of the almighty dollar," as Pierre put it wryly, to serve their community. The ROC found them at this opportune moment.

Many other ROC members played essential roles in steering the ROC: Angela and Kevin Doyle, Diane and Philip Powell, Yvette Lynch, Greg Humbert, Kathy Kelly, Kelda Whalen, Michèle Gascon, and others. Though we were unable to interview all members, the following stories derive from each of their efforts. Whether they served for a year or twenty, all members contributed to the foundation of activism that has supported the ROC's work for thirty years and counting.

* * *

Early ROC members knew they had a great deal to learn about refugee and newcomer experiences as they launched themselves into their new work. As of 1990, only a few members had experience with newcomer services in Ottawa. Louise was serving on the CCI's board of directors as secretary. She and Kevin and Angela Doyle were already active volunteers in the CCI's host program. All three had some limited experience with assisting newcomers to enroll their children in school, find a doctor, and open a bank account—as well as with co-signing leases and providing friendship and respectful counsel in other facets of daily life in Canada.

In November 1990, Louise enlisted the help of Norma McCord, CCI's new host program coordinator, to provide training to this new committee in the making. Norma had been working with Ottawa's refugee-serving groups and organizations since 1980, during Project 4000. Within the month, Norma matched each of the ROC members with a family to host, including families from Bangladesh, El Salvador, Ethiopia, Nicaragua, and Uganda.

Hosting

Louise hoped that hosting would help the nascent ROC's members gain cross-cultural experience and learn how to welcome newcomers to Ottawa. The early benefit of hosting was that it did not carry the same financial responsibilities and time commitment as private sponsorship. Norma McCord recalls that a benefit of the CCI's host program was that it gave groups institutional support: "The nice thing about hosting was ... people who were nervous about taking on these big responsibilities had somebody: there was a settlement worker if you had a question."

Developing friendships with people from all over the world exposed ROC members to a range of settlement issues most of them had never anticipated. As they met with refuge-seekers and immigrants in their homes, ROC members were placed in a unique position to hear and see first-hand what settlement services and support they were lacking in the local community. In 1992, Margo Gauthier began visiting a young Salvadoran man with Louise through the host program. On one of her visits, Margo and her husband, Pierre, noticed that the man's home was almost entirely bare. He had no table, bed, chairs or sofa. Realizing that this could be easily remedied, Pierre and Margo placed an ad in the Parish bulletin requesting furniture donations for the ROC. The Parish's response was positive and within weeks, the man's apartment was completely outfitted.

With this small success under their belt, other ROC members began to notice that many families they hosted were also in need of furniture or appliances. Since parishioners were still calling in with donations, the Gauthiers offered to continue gathering used furniture to meet the needs of newcomer families. They soon established a system they called the Furniture Pick-up and Delivery Service: the ROC would gather information on the needs of the newcomers and refuge-seekers they knew in the community and then they would advertise in the Parish bulletin for the pieces that were needed.

In organic and incremental ways, ROC members, parishioners, and community members pitched in with ideas to improve this service. Margo, who had previous experience as an office manager, was especially good at orchestrating furniture pick-ups and drop-offs. She loved to find the perfect pieces for newcomers' homes, when possible, colour coordinating the wall paint, the sofa, and the drapes and cushions. Margo and Pierre believed that friendly delivery of furniture could go a long way in helping refugees feel welcome in the community.

Since the Parish had no storage facility, at first the Parish's Oblate priests allowed them to store furniture in a building they owned. When the building was sold, Pierre and others would ask parishioners to keep their donations until they had a home for them. One parishioner, Adrian Van den Brock, spent many hours hauling furniture with his pick-up truck.

ROC members also learned to question their own assumptions and to be more aware of the cultural differences they might encounter. One day Pierre and Margo visited an Afghan family with five children in their small, immaculately tidy home. The family asked if the ROC could help them acquire a carpet. Though Pierre said he would try, he noticed that the family did not have a table and said he could easily bring them one. They accepted and a few weeks later Pierre returned with a new carpet and table. As a thank you, the family invited the couple over for Sunday dinner. To Pierre's surprise, when everyone sat down together to eat, the family served dinner on the carpet.

On another occasion, Pierre and Margo acted as hosts to a Yugoslav family. The father of the family asked if he could help him find a desk for his home. Pierre recalls, ruefully, that he had thought the man "a bit of a pain" when he offered him a table and the man insisted on a desk. Later Pierre learned that before coming to Canada as a refugee, the man had been an electronics engineer. Since his arrival in Canada, he had been spending his days reading whatever material he could get a hold of to bring himself up to date with the Canadian market. A desk was an important factor in this plan. The man eventually found a job in his field and had a successful career. He and Pierre keep in touch to this day. Pierre carried with him the lessons about the assumptions he had made as he came to know more refuge-seekers and immigrants over the years.

The Furniture Pick-up and Delivery Service became the ROC's unofficial publicity agent, as frequent requests for furniture in the Parish bulletin drew the attention of parishioners and connected them with newcomers. The used furniture service also allowed the ROC to strengthen its connections with other ministries at St. Joe's Parish. Parishioners and leaders knew they could call on the Gauthiers if they knew of someone in their community who might have similar needs. They also developed cooperative partnerships with St. Vincent de Paul, a thrift store in Ottawa on Wellington Street, which allowed the ROC to trade in any furniture or household items they received for an in-store credit.

In 1998, the ROC estimated having undertaken 635 pick-ups and deliveries in the previous year, with excesses going to St. Vincent de Paul for credits totalling eight thousand dollars. The Furniture Pick-up and Delivery Service continued until 2008, for a total of sixteen years. By 2002, the Gauthiers had stepped back a little to limit deliveries to the most essential requests. When the demand began to exceed Pierre and Margo's capacities, they were able to withdraw, knowing their work would be continued by a newly established non-profit called Helping with Furniture (HWF), started by Nathalie Mayone and Buffy Cassidy in 2005, which began as a service to provide gently used furniture and household goods to refugees and refugee claimants. Though a little more geographically restricted than Pierre and Margo's ad hoc furniture pick-up and delivery service, HWF still exists today and was instrumental in supporting the many Syrian refugees who arrived in Ottawa throughout 2016 and 2017 (Mills 2016).

Hosting also taught the ROC how quickly newcomers must become proficient in one of Canada's two official languages. Indeed, language barriers sometimes made it difficult for ROC members to develop their relationships with newcomers. Many of the newcomers or refuge-seekers they were matched with initially spoke little English or French, and most ROC members only spoke English. Over time, they learned to navigate language barriers in a variety of creative ways. Though they were rarely able to pay for professional interpreters, they could occasionally rely on volunteers if they could find someone within the Parish or among friends who spoke the necessary language (Spanish, Bengali, Farsi, French, etc.). If volunteers could not be there in person to interpret, they would occasionally join by phone.

ROC members also witnessed newcomers' challenges with employment and language acquisition. They found that language acquisition was a near essential prerequisite for employment and for integration into their new community. One Nicaraguan family of four, with limited English, struggled for over a year to find work. Meanwhile, the father of a Salvadoran family found a job after only six months as a Spanish-speaking correspondent for Radio Canada International, due to his fluency in English.

After a number of conversations with newcomers in the host program, the ROC recognized that they could help with this language transition. In 1994, St. Joe's collaborated with four other churches (Calvary Baptist, Canadian Martyrs, Church of the Ascension, and Wesley United) to establish a drop-in English Conversation Group (ECG) for refugees and immigrants on Wednesday evenings. It was the first volunteer program of its kind in Ottawa, free to anyone who showed up. It was completely run by volunteers. With an annual operating budget of a thousand dollars, the group rented out a basement room once a week in an apartment building located at 170 Lees Avenue, which was home to many immigrant families. Residents could conveniently start a load of laundry before going next door to participate in lively conversation.

The ECG allowed newcomers, immigrants and refugees, to practise one-on-one conversation with volunteers in a low-pressure environment. They would also role-play in groups, for example, pretending to interview for a job or buy materials in a hardware store.

At first, ROC members took turns attending and facilitating the sessions with their ecumenical partners. However, in 1994, this became unnecessary when a new parishioner, named Greg Humbert, moved to Ottawa and began to volunteer on behalf of the ROC at the ECG. He quickly became part of the core coordinating team, along with Pat Barr from St. Joe's and Haig McCarrell from St. Albans, the Anglican church on King Edward Avenue.

Greg also gained a deep appreciation for the challenges refugees and immigrants face when coming to Canada. He was humbled to realize that many of the ECG's attendees were doctors and professionals in their home countries who had left everything behind to seek safety or start anew with their families. When attendees became discouraged that they would never learn English, Greg would tell them the story of his friend, a Bosnian woman who had arrived at the ECG only knowing "yes" and "thank you." After two years of practice, her English enabled her to land a job at the National Archives of Canada.

ECG volunteers became close friends with many of the regular attendees. After their Wednesday classes, Greg, Pat, and Haig frequently went to movies and brought along their newcomer friends. They held picnics and Christmas parties. As Pat Barr told a journalist in 2005, "Friendship is a natural outcome of these encounters" (ROC Archives 2006). Greg believes this was possible because the ECG was unencumbered by bureaucracy, membership dues, or mandatory attendance.

The ECG eventually became independent from the ROC, and Greg remained with the group for thirteen years. It still operates today, despite periods when the group had fewer regular volunteers or attendees. Yet people would inevitably "come out of the wood-work," Greg remembers.

Relationships that developed through the ROC host program, furniture delivery, and the ECG were, in many circumstances, deeply reciprocal and long lasting. A woman who came to Canada seeking refuge from South Sudan remembers:

> It's tough to be a newcomer in a country where you don't know the language, the culture, and the system. [Louise] helped me to learn English and showed me where to get information. She found good schools for the children.... She was always there for me. She gave her heart to me. All she did, I will never forget.... Now I am doing things I thought I could never do. (ROC Archives 2007)

In response, Louise turned the story back to the value she received from hosting her friend and the family:

> As the host, what do I say about the experience of welcoming and befriending this family? I say that I got more out of the relation-ship than they did. I learned to understand and respect their culture and be enriched by it. I learned that simple things can bring great joy, that life need not be complicated. They have become loyal friends. I truly appreciate [that friendship]. And Canada has been enriched. It is a better country for having given this family a home. (ROC Archives 2007)

The years of experience ROC members gained through hosting taught them essential lessons about treating refuge-seekers and newcomers with dignity and respect. They learned to cast aside their assump-tions or expectations, to give the refugees they supported room to make their own choices, and to allow them to set the terms of the relationship.

Private Sponsorship

The ROC was just getting started with hosting when, in early December of 1990, they received an urgent request from Bernie Walsh, CCI's private sponsorship coordinator. Since the 1978 *Immigration Act* and the 1970s' Southeast Asian refugee project, the federal government had continued to allow Canadians and permanent residents—often through faith or community groups—to fully fund and support a refugee, or refugee family, for their first year in Canada. CCI had committed to sponsor a young Eritrean man named Tesfay. The problem was that Tesfay would be arriving in Canada six weeks ahead of schedule and no one was lined up to welcome him.

The ROC was hesitant to launch right into private sponsorship prior to gaining any hosting experience, but Bernie explained that he had reached out to three other Catholic parishes and none were in a financial position to receive Tesfay on such short notice. Surprised and anxious, but willing to try, the ROC spoke to their parish leadership and gained their support in the form of a three-thousand-dollar loan. All this occurred within a few days.

Tesfay arrived in Ottawa on December 7, after spending two years in Italy as an asylum seeker. Because his status in Italy was uncertain, the organization Caritas helped to connect him with Ottawa's CCI for sponsorship. As his sponsors, the ROC quickly rallied around him. They invited him to their Christmas celebrations, got him settled into his apartment, and helped him to register for language instruction for new Canadians (LINC) classes.[1] Tesfay's monthly expenses were approximately five hundred dollars (three hundred for rent, a hundred and sixty for food, and forty for bus fare). However, at the time, a government-training program paid newly arrived refugees four hundred dollars a month to take LINC classes for their first six months. This meant the ROC only had to help him with about a hundred dollars a month.

To the delight of the ROC, by March, Tesfay was keeping up in his LINC classes and had found a part-time job cleaning offices at

---

1   LINC classes at the time were known as ESL (English as a second language) classes. It was eventually realized that newcomers frequently already spoke more than one language, so the English they were learning might be their third—or even their fourth or fifth—language, so the terminology was updated. However, the term ESL reflected the common assumptions of unilingual anglophones at the time.

night. Having secured additional income to supplement his LINC funding, he no longer required the ROC's financial assistance. As sponsors, they continued supporting him with friendship, advice, and sometimes furniture and transportation, as he settled into his new life. They remember him as a "reserved, refined and unassuming young man." For many years to come, Louise frequented the Horn of Africa restaurant where Tesfay worked in the kitchen. He would sit and keep her company as she ate. He later moved to the apartment building where Louise was a tenant. They continued to cross paths for many years to come.

In the years following, private sponsorship was not the ROC's primary activity. They recognized that the demand for sponsorship often exceeded their capacity: fundraising could be challenging and time consuming, because, at that time, parishioners were not so actively interested in refugee issues. Yet, after their experience with Tesfay, the ROC recognized that private sponsorship was a way for their small group to make a big difference. As a consequence, they frequently found themselves taking on urgent sponsorships when they received requests from partners in the community. Additionally, as ROC members began to host refugees from all over the world, they learned about family members still living in precarious situations who would also benefit from resettlement in Canada.

Between 1991 and 1992, the ROC received nine requests for private sponsorship. As early as January of 1991, they laid out rules for discerning the order in which to address requests for assistance. The rules included prioritizing refugees "in life threatening situations, those whose survival was at a high risk, and those who were vulnerable and in need of protection" (ROC Archives 1991).

In the summer of 1991, the ROC received an urgent sponsorship request they felt bound to honour. The ROC had previously hosted a man named Akello who had gained a bit of notoriety in the community for aiding the Ottawa police in the arrest of a shoplifter. One day, already very ill, he was sitting in his wheelchair in front of a store when he saw a man running out with his arms full of clothes, pursued by the shopkeeper. Akello tripped the man and the police were able to catch him. Following the incident, he was proud to show the award he had been given by Ottawa police. Louise was invited to the award ceremony.

Sadly, in 1991, Akello was diagnosed with a terminal illness. He pleaded with the ROC to sponsor a family member so that he would not die alone. The ROC raised eight thousand dollars and, with a letter of support from Akello's family doctor, a brother who had sought refuge in Botswana arrived in September 1992, less than a year after the sponsorship application was submitted. Although the brothers did not get along as well as expected, they were able to see each other before Akello passed away four months later.

Beginning in 1993, in part due to an economic downturn, the ROC abandoned the idea of privately sponsoring refugees. The ongoing recession dimmed the prospects of successful fundraising within the Parish. As well, a reduction in federal and provincial funding for settlement services put even more pressure on volunteer organizations to take on the tasks and costs of settlement.

The ROC only returned to sponsorship in 1999 when the ROC formed a partnership with a religious congregation of women called Religious of the Sacred Heart of Jesus (RSCJ)—an order of Catholic sisters located around the world and present in Ottawa since 1978 (Baudoin 1981). The agreement was that the RSCJ would provide the funds for a private sponsorship and the ROC would assume the responsibility of settling a family in Canada over the course of their first year. Together, they applied to sponsor a family from Equatorial Guinea who had resided in France for two years. The family had been in France on student visas when a military coup in Equatorial Guinea occurred. Their efforts to extend their status in France were unsuccessful. The family was eventually connected with the RSCJ in Paris and appealed to them for help. The RSCJ in Paris turned to their co-members in Montreal and were eventually connected with the ROC.

In the end, the Equatorial Guinean family cancelled their sponsorship application to Canada because they were offered residence in France. However, this episode helped the ROC to recognize the value of developing connections and networks with persistent and caring migrant advocates. The RSCJ and the ROC eventually did partner again to submit another sponsorship application for an Iranian couple living without legal status in Thailand, which was ultimately successful in 2000.

In another collaboration, in May of 2000, the ROC teamed up with the First Unitarian Church in Ottawa to undertake a Joint Assistance Sponsorship (JAS) to quickly bring to Canada an Iranian "woman at risk" named Farah and her eight-year-old son named Ervin. JAS, a partnership between the Government of Canada and community members, was new to the ROC; they learned that the program allowed the Canadian government to fast-track the resettlement of refugees who require significant support. As is done for GARs, the settlement costs for JAS refuge-seekers are typically fully funded by the federal government. But because of their higher needs, JAS refuge-seekers also require support from a group of community members to help with their day-to-day settlement issues, in the same way that PSRs are supported. Support for JAS refuge-seekers also lasts for a longer period of time, sometimes up to 36 months. JAS refuge-seekers require additional support for a number of possible reasons, potentially related to violence or torture, medical disabilities, the effects of systemic discrimination, or simply having a very large family. Women at risk is one category of JAS refuge-seekers.

Again, the family arrived quickly, within a few weeks of the JAS agreement being signed, and the ROC assigned sponsorship and settlement tasks. They helped register Farah for English classes and registered Ervin, her bright, active son, for school and swimming lessons. ROC members took them grocery shopping and to the library, helped them get a telephone hooked up, get health cards, and many other practical tasks that are challenging for newcomers.

In a newsletter to the Parish, the ROC wrote:

> [I]t has not all been business: celebration has been a central part of this sponsorship! [Farah] arrived the day after her birthday, and we brought her flowers in keeping with the Canadian custom of attention to birthdays.... [Farah and Ervin] both enjoyed bikes this summer thanks to the generosity of the parishioners. Tours of the city, outings to a cottage, an Iranian film at the [Bytowne Cinema].... New bonds of understanding and friendship are building, and sponsorship has proven to be a mutually enriching outreach for all partners. (ROC Archives 2000)

It became easier for the ROC to engage in private sponsorship beginning in 2001, when CCI began managing a newly signed sponsorship agreement between the federal government and the Archdiocese of Ottawa. In Canada, incorporated organizations are permitted to sign an agreement with the Minister of Immigration, Refugees and Citizenship to resettle refugees from abroad. Organizations that sign such agreements are called Sponsorship Agreement Holders (SAHs) and are frequently faith-based, ethnic, community, or humanitarian organizations. They are given the responsibility to manage smaller community sponsor groups known as Constituent Groups (CGs). CGs are frequently local faith congregations that take on the financial and settlement responsibilities of a sponsorship. SAHs and CGs provide a valuable service to the government. With years of experience assessing eligibility and admissibility criteria, SAHs can help to reduce the number of ineligible applicants or mistakes in the paperwork by pre-screening applications. And CGs provide hours of settlement support at no cost. Throughout the sponsorships, SAHs provide CGs with expertise, advice, information, support, and monitoring.

St. Joe's ROC was able to take advantage of CCI's role as the manager of the Archdiocese's SAH to become a CG. As a CG, the ROC could co-sponsor refugees with community members. Individuals and groups from the community began approaching them to sponsor friends or family members abroad. For instance, in 2001, Father McDonald of the Archdiocese of Ottawa learned of Prahan, a Canadian originally from Sri Lanka, living in Toronto, who had a brother he wished to sponsor. Prahan's brother had fled to India and was given refugee status by the UNHCR. Prahan and three other people provided the funds for his settlement, while the ROC helped to prepare the application.

Just as the ROC began looking at taking on a number of additional co-sponsorships, the terrorist attacks of September 11, 2001, brought about swift change. After 9/11 fear over security framed the debate on immigration and refugee intake and cast suspicion on migrants from everywhere.

The impulse to frame migrants, including refugees and asylum seekers, as a security risk has an unfortunately long history in Canada and globally (Whitaker 1987; Watson 2007). Moments of crisis—9/11, as a paradigmatic example, but also irregular arrivals, or foreign wars—can spur the adoption of harsh policies toward migrants, including increased use of detention, expedited refugee hearings, and reduced procedural guarantees (Lenard and Macdonald 2019; Atak, Hudson, and Nakache 2018). All this, despite the fact that history shows that concerns migrants pose a security threat or that they are, in general, a source of violence or crime are rarely warranted (e.g., Amuedo-Dorantes, Bansak, and Pozo 2021; Masterson and Yasenov 2019).

Refugees were increasingly expected to demonstrate that they knew their Canadian sponsors. This was difficult for religious groups like the ROC to prove because they often received sponsorship referrals from people in the community. In February of 2003, Irene Kellow wrote an article for the parish newsletter, *The Spirit*, saying, "The prospects of [refugees] getting admitted to Canada have diminished as all aspects of sponsorships are subject to even greater scrutiny" (ROC Archives 2003).

These changes prevented the ROC from pursuing several sponsorships they had wanted to undertake. Still, due to their ingenuity and experience with the different avenues of sponsorship, the ROC found ways to work around them. Irene recalls a time soon after 9/11 when an Ethiopian woman was referred to her, hoping to bring one of her relatives to Canada. Since the ROC did not know this woman personally, they felt they could not support the application. Irene suggested that the ROC invite her to become a member, with the condition that she remain and participate for a year; they would then be positioned to vouch for her family members. The woman joined and became an active member of the group. At the end of the year, as they prepared to submit a sponsorship application, the person was suddenly accepted for resettlement in the US and the ROC's assistance was no longer required.

Cancelled sponsorships were not uncommon, and the ROC's efforts to sponsor were frequently thwarted. Each case had a different reason. Some ended early when the ROC gathered information and discovered that the person did not qualify for refugee status after all and, therefore, was not eligible for resettlement. Some ended after years of work, with applications refused for security reasons or the person being offered asylum elsewhere. Some were heartbreaking for the ROC, such as when they applied to sponsor seven Ugandan orphans to help them come live with their aunt, their closest living relative, in Canada. They were refused for not having refugee status. Some were bittersweet, such as their application in 1999 for the family from Equatorial Guinea that ended up being granted asylum in France.

ROC members began to understand how the spirit and patience of refugee applicants could be sorely tested. After an initial interview, refugees had to undergo a health test and then a security check, which could take up to a year. If the security check exceeded a year, then the health check would have to be repeated. Taking all these factors into consideration, the ROC learned to expect private sponsorships to take up to two years of processing. Such a delay meant that the ROC, and any other private sponsorship groups in Canada, had to be incredibly stable. Even if the group was stable, many other obstacles might delay or cancel a private sponsorship over those two years.

The ROC persevered, however, and managed three successful private sponsorships in the late 2000s, including for a family of six from Myanmar in 2006, a young Nigerian girl in 2008, and a young woman from Eritrea also in 2008. The sponsorship in 2008 introduced the ROC to a whole new range of needs. The CCI urgently requested that a group take on a JAS for a Nigerian "woman at risk," a fifteen-year-old girl who had been trafficked in Europe. In spite of the greater responsibility of sponsoring a minor, the ROC accepted and, since "women at risk" candidates are fast-tracked, the girl, Sheba, arrived in Ottawa in less than a week.

One can only imagine how it might have felt for Sheba to arrive alone at the Ottawa airport, with little knowledge of what or who awaited her. Sheba recalls that due to the traumatic circumstances of her displacement, she worried about meeting her sponsors. She remembers thinking that if her sponsors were young people, she would run away. How surprised she was when she reached the top of the escalator and looked down to find a group of "older people" awaiting her in the arrival area: "It was Margo. Margo [had a] sign and had a parcel with my name.... It actually gave me a sense of peace, knowing that there's no way that these older people are going to treat me bad in any way."

The ROC helped Sheba get settled into Carty House, a communal residence that provides transitional housing for female refuge-seekers in Ottawa, for her first year. She remembers thinking that life in Canada would be perfect and that everything would work out. She quickly realized that, although things were not always perfect, she had gotten, in her words, "really, really lucky to have St. Joe's Parish." She felt immediately enveloped by their desire to help her, to get her going, and to convince her that everything would work out.

The ROC helped her find a wonderful family doctor. Not only was the doctor female, which made Sheba more comfortable, but she had also worked in Africa and had experience that helped her to understand Sheba's particular trauma. The ROC also helped Sheba find a high school, and members picked her up each morning to take her there. She felt comforted knowing that though she was in a new country on her own, she had people she could rely on and turn to when needed. The ROC frequently reminded her, "You can call us at any time," and she learned that it was true. If she called, they would answer.

She also grew to love the faith community of St. Joe's Parish as a whole. She told us, "You don't have to be a Catholic to go to

St. Joe's. ... We welcome you just the way you are. ... If you feel that you belong here, we're going to support you just to know that you belong here."

Twelve years later, Sheba still sees Pierre Gauthier as a father figure and mentor. They speak often to this day. She told us, "Pierre has the biggest personality. ... I don't know what Canada would have been like if I didn't have people like [him]." Pierre proudly told us: "She is bright and determined. ... So I've got an adopted daughter who is twenty-eight or so and she works for [Company]." He listed off her accomplishments and added, "When you get involved with refugees, you end up creating a family of a kind."

Mercy, another PSR from Eritrea, arrived in 2008. She recounts a similar story about arriving at the Ottawa airport late at night. On the plane ride she met another young woman, also Eritrean, and who was being sponsored by her uncle in Canada. As they walked through the airport, Mercy told this new friend how she felt afraid of what her new life would bring. Her new friend asked her, "Who is going to come to get you?" and she responded, "My sponsor. I know their names, but I don't know their faces." When they came down the escalator, her new friend explained, "Mercy! That's your name there." Louise was standing at the bottom of the stairs with Mercy's name written on a sign. Looking back on this moment, Mercy's voice fills with emotion: "I can't even say. She's like a mom. I didn't feel like I was coming to someone I don't know."

Mercy also lived in Carty House in the beginning. Over the following months, she went with Louise everywhere. To her, Louise was like a mother. She remembers Louise saying, "Mercy, I'm here for you," and she knew it was true. Mercy's quiet personality made her hesitant to reach out for help, but the ROC members continued to encourage her to talk with them and with the other women staying in Carty House. After three months, she became comfortable enough with the buses to make her own way around the city to visit new friends and run errands. Parishioners welcomed her into their homes for Thanksgiving and Christmas, which helped her feel less lonely. Eventually, the ROC helped to bring her husband, whom she had married shortly before leaving Eritrea, to Canada. With advice from the ROC, Mercy and her husband were eventually even able to sponsor her two brothers and sister-in-law, who now live in Canada with their children. Mercy now has three children of her own and is in regular contact with Louise to this day.

Refugee Claimants

Early on, a number of ROC members, and Marg Quinn in particular, recognized that if they were to serve those in need, they had to be able to reach *all* kinds of refuge-seekers, including refugee claimants (also often referred to as asylum seekers). Refugee claimants are those who file claims for protection upon arriving in Canada. They may do so at land borders, airports, ports, inland immigration offices, etc. As they await their hearings with the Immigration and Refugee Board (IRB), they face unique challenges, since politicians and the public sometimes mistakenly portray the means by which they arrive in Canada as illegal, presenting them as queue jumpers, casting doubt on their stories of persecution, and causing stigmatization (Showler 2006).

Crossing a border to make a refugee claim is legal in countries that have ratified the *Refugee Convention* and implemented it in domestic laws as Canada has through its *Immigration and Refugee Protection Act* (IRPA). Inconsistencies in Canadian immigration law, however, have given rise to contradictory legal frameworks in the IRPA. Assumptions made about the ineligibility of refugee claimants are easy enough for the IRB to uphold through the group of laws that make up the IRPA, whether through the exclusion framework denying refugee status or the inadmissibility framework dealing with various types of criminality (Bond, Benson, and Porter 2020). Refugee claimants are especially vulnerable to the legal discrepancies that make Canada's refugee system inconsistent with the *Refugee Convention* (Bond, Benson, and Porter 2020; Bond 2016). In light of these conditions, refugee claimants benefit greatly from advocacy and legal representation throughout the asylum process. Furthermore, the ability of asylum seekers to appeal IRB decisions that run contrary to the *Refugee Convention* is essential in refugee claimant cases. However, as Chapters 2 and 3 explain, the right to appeal is recent, and was achieved, in part, due to ROC advocacy.

Early ROC members believed that they could provide support and friendship to refugee claimants that would help reduce some of the challenges they experienced upon arrival. However, the ROC faced a number of obstacles to helping those seeking refuge in this way. First, CCI's mandate did not include providing services to refugee claimants in Ottawa. Since the ROC relied on referrals from CCI, especially in its early years, it was harder to connect with refugee claimants. Another obstacle in the ROC's relationship with refugee claimants was the misgivings of some of its members, knowing that refugee claimants remain in Canada under very uncertain conditions. Since refugee claimants are only entitled to remain in Canada as long as their claims have not yet been processed or rejected, the nature of their stay is more precarious. ROC members found it difficult to predict the length and level of support a refugee claimant might need.

Notwithstanding these challenges, Marg Quinn pushed the ROC in 1994 to specifically earmark four thousand five hundred dollars for assisting three refugee claimants that year. They agreed they would provide financial assistance on an ad hoc basis for single claimants rather than families.

On a wintery day in 1994, Yvette Lynch and Irene Kellow drove to the old Voyageur bus station in Ottawa to welcome one of the first refugee claimants they ever helped: Fabrice. Fabrice was from Zaïre (now the Democratic Republic of Congo) and spoke French. He had been referred to them from Toronto, where Marg was in contact with Mary Jo Leddy, an activist who operated (and still operates) the Romero House for refugee claimants. Occasionally Romero House received French-speaking claimants whom Mary Jo referred to Marg because she felt that they might be more comfortable in Ottawa. When they met Fabrice, Irene remembers he was unprepared for the cold Ottawa weather. She had brought him a sweater to keep him warm on their way to drop him off at the YMCA. Irene later put out a call to her colleagues at work for winter clothes, which yielded two smart ski outfits.

To get to know Fabrice and to show him the city, Yvette and Marg arranged an outing to Winterlude, Ottawa's winter festival, to show him the ice sculptures and the frozen canal. Yvette later wrote:

> All my efforts to describe Winterlude in my somewhat limited French were greeted with guarded enthusiasm, until I mentioned walking on the lake. There was a pause, he was not sure that I was serious and could not fathom how we could possibly walk on a lake. ... At Dow's Lake we stood at the pavilion watching the skaters and other people enjoying the activities, and though there was still some apprehension, I could see a little optimism emerging. About three minutes onto the lake he was making skating motions with his hands and feet and saying that this was not so bad ... he could even try skating sometime. (ROC Archives 1997)

The ROC's challenge in finding refugee claimants to assist eventually solved itself. For one, CCI began to recognize that though it did not have a mandate to serve refugee claimants, the ROC had greater liberty to do so and they began referring people to the ROC for assistance. Other refugee claimants were introduced to ROC members by parishioners and friends. The ROC helped with whatever services they could: for some, they provided furniture; for others, they provided loans for legal fees; and with many more, they shared friendship and advice when necessary.

Pierre and Margo Gauthier became especially close with a young woman named Madeleine from Cameroon, who arrived in Ottawa in 2003 as a refugee claimant with her two young boys and pregnant with a third. She was referred to the ROC by Dr. Donna Bowers, who had met Madeleine when she had come into her office for a prenatal examination. Serendipitously, Dr. Bowers was a member of St. Joe's Parish and knew about the ROC's services. After chatting for a bit, Dr. Bowers asked the young woman if she would be willing to talk to Louise.

A few days later, Louise and Madeleine spoke on the phone and arranged to meet. Pierre accompanied Louise. Pierre and the young woman soon struck up what was to become a deep and lasting friendship. Margo and Pierre Gauthier co-signed Madeleine's lease to her first apartment in Ottawa; through the ROC, they helped collect donations of furniture, clothes, and food for her and her kids; and they provided friendship and emotional support as she adjusted to her new life. Madeleine remembers how helpful their advice was to her early days in Canada: "They really assisted me in all ways. ... After a few months, I felt I had been in Canada for ten years." She recounts a story of a time, just two weeks after giving birth to her third son. She was at home and her eldest was outside riding his bike. He tried to go off a jump and fell, breaking his arm. Madeleine called 9-1-1 and then immediately called Pierre, who came over as quickly as he could. He arrived just in time to get into the ambulance with her son so that she could stay with her baby.

Years later, the family continued to attend St. Joe's and the boys were baptized there. They eventually moved to British Columbia, but fifteen years later, in 2019, at Margo's passing, Madeleine flew back to Ottawa with her eldest son to attend her celebration of life.

The CCI also helped connect Irene with two female refugee claimants, one originally from Ghana and the other from Zimbabwe.

Both women had young children and Irene and Yvette began meeting with them frequently to talk about their careers, raising their children, and adjusting to life in Canada. Pierre and Irene got very involved in collecting furniture and other items for their respective homes, and the pair even accompanied one of them to her refugee hearing, and later, to her citizenship ceremony. Eventually, Yvette, Pierre, and Irene became godparents to the three children. Three years after meeting members of the ROC, the woman from Ghana wrote in a letter:

> Thank you very much for your kindness over these last three years. Your organization makes a world of difference in the lives of immigrants. When my kids and I immigrated to Canada, we did not know what to expect—having crossed paths with some of your members it sure has made for a smooth transition. ... Thanks for being part of our extended family! (ROC Archives 2004)

* * *

From 1990 until 2008, the ROC provided friendship and support to people from nearly every war or conflict zone of that time: Afghanistan, Bangladesh, Bosnia, El Salvador, Ethiopia, Guatemala, Iran, Iraq, Nicaragua, Russia, Rwanda, Somalia, Sri Lanka, Sudan, Uganda, and more. Their positive experiences—with the host program and private sponsorship—helped the ROC determine how to implement its mission and to discern which activities would become their focus. It also established the ROC's close partnership with CCI, which, itself, was in the process of establishing its identity. The benefit of this partnership was that the ROC was never short of opportunities to serve; the CCI counted on the ROC, and it delegated requests for assistance to it. These requests helped the ROC to maintain momentum in their early years.

Looking back on the ROC's successes, it is clear that their actions were at times extraordinary. Taking on sponsorships at the very last minute and delivering 635 pieces of furniture in a year are indeed extraordinary actions, as are spending hours each week meeting with and assisting newcomers, driving them around the city, filling out paperwork, sharing holidays, and developing lasting friendships. However, ROC members deflect any praise for these actions, because they view themselves as ordinary.

When speaking about why they stayed on the ROC for so many years, many emphasized the mutual friendships they developed. Some said that they never intended to get so involved but that once they knew the people they were serving, they fell in love with the work. When referring to their religious and spiritual reasons for doing the work, ROC members said things like, "Christianity is our motivation, but we are not here to proselytize."

ROC members were also deeply motivated by the belief that contact with private individuals could help newcomers settle more quickly and comfortably in Canada. Research suggests that this is true: studies show that PSRs, meaning refugees who receive settlement support from private sponsors, attain "slightly quicker self-sufficiency" than those resettled by the government (GARs). PSRs find employment more quickly and earn higher wages in the short term, even after controlling for differences in education, language ability, and other socio-demographic factors (Kaida, Hou, and Stick 2020). This is positive evidence for community-based refugee resettlement, which focuses on pairing refuge-seekers with private individuals, whether directly through private sponsorship or through host programs, to establish friendships and a sense of community. Even when sponsors' formal support ends one year after arrival, many refuge-seekers maintain ties with their sponsors, which can be a benefit to both parties for years to come (Aylesworth and Ossorio 1983; Neuwirth and Clark 1981). The close relationships and communication channels between ROC members and the individuals and families they supported facilitated many families' early years of integration and continue to add value to their lives to this day.

Over these early years, the ROC learned to avoid mistakes that newer groups and volunteers occasionally make when embarking in settlement work. They knew that it is often best to only sign a lease after a family's arrival, since approval or travel often ends up being delayed and apartments sit empty. They learned to navigate the delicate balance between providing advice and letting refuge-seekers make their own decisions. They learned how to tap into community resources to build their capacity. As Chapter 2 shows, these lessons were essential in 2005 when the ROC chose to participate in one of their most extraordinary acts yet: the provision of sanctuary, in collaboration with another parish, to a refugee claimant whose application for refugee status had been rejected by the federal government.

The ROC's many years of service was only possible because of the recruitment of a number of individuals capable of investing a great deal of time and energy in the Committee, even while working full-time. Retired parishioners in particular could more flexibly devote themselves to the ROC's initiatives, such as furniture delivery, or taking on leadership roles. Louise was able to dedicate so many years to the ROC in part because of her position as a member of a Catholic Secular Institute. A number of other long-time ROC members were young retirees, including Pierre, Margo, and Marg.

Additionally, ROC members relied on maintaining the strong professional and friendly relationships they developed with each other. They became an unconventional family. Like any group working together on complex issues and long-term projects, the ROC experienced regular interpersonal conflicts. A number of members had strong opinions and different approaches. Some made deep and lasting connections with the refuge-seekers they served, becoming like family. Some preferred coordinating finances and logistics. However, Committee members found that despite their differences they were all deeply committed to the ROC's mission. Their shared values kept them together over time. They found out that the ROC was large enough for each person to have some autonomy and to take on the roles that best suited their skills and interests. Later, if members were burned out or overwhelmed, they were able to step back and let others take the lead.

Since it was a parish with a significant focus on social justice, having the ROC as one of St. Joe's outreach ministries was a natural fit. It seems incredibly vital, also, that the ROC was built upon institutional relationships and structures that propelled their work. St. Joe's leadership certainly empowered the ROC to fulfill its purpose with institutional support. Father Robert Smith OMI, St. Joe's Parish priest in the mid-1990s, was very interested in refugee issues and attended many of the ROC's meetings. At one point when the ROC had no active cases, he kindly chided them saying they could hardly call themselves "a refugee group" if they had no direct involvement with refugees. They quickly remedied the situation. Rosemary Williams recalls the Parish leadership's support: "There was no blocking. In fact, there was a real collaborative sense. At the same time, we were allowed to be quite independent and define ourselves." However, the Parish gave them a place to meet, to recruit members, to fundraise, and to seek parishioner support when needs arose.

Additionally, the ROC's connection with CCI, as a Catholic community service, gave them access to training and an established network of services to facilitate their work. CCI staff were strong refugee advocates—Julie Salach-Simard, for instance, CCI's SAH coordinator. For years, Julie helped the ROC with sponsorship applications and paperwork and was always available to help them with the formalities and logistics of refugee hosting and sponsorship. Irene remembers, "She was a great source of inspiration and information." It was Julie who pointed them toward a number of refugee claimants over the years, even though CCI's mandate and government funding did not extend to claimants. Julie was the one to connect Irene with the two refugee claimant women from Ghana and Zimbabwe. She had asked Irene to go to the YMCA to introduce herself to the young Ghanaian mother and later provided them with tickets to the Shriner's circus and invited them to CCI's annual picnic. In turn, the ROC members' willingness to volunteer their time as hosts and sponsors made the Parish-supported Committee a valuable asset to CCI. CCI relied on the ROC over the years, as they did in the above mentioned situations, with hosting, and in emergency sponsorships—in December of 1990 with the young Eritrean man or in 2008 with Sheba from Nigeria.

The stories of the ROC's first fifteen years—from hosting to private sponsorship to ad hoc services for other newcomers in Ottawa—are foundational to the work that was accomplished in the next fifteen years. As the testimonies of refuge-seekers demonstrate in this chapter, the actions of ROC members were significant and meaningful to many. Small actions by individuals—alone and as part of a group—can have huge impacts. In Chapters 2 and 3, we explore how the ROC's foundational lessons resonated for years to come and prepared them for advocacy on a national stage. In Chapter 4, we explore how these years of experience positioned ROC members as experts in settlement during Ottawa's—and Canada's—initiative to resettle thousands of Syrian refugees in 2015.

CHAPTER 2

Advocacy through Sanctuary

B y the 2000s, with over a decade of experience, St. Joe's Refugee Outreach Committee (ROC) had found its place within Ottawa's settlement services. In their day-to-day tasks, Committee members cooperated with the Catholic Centre for Immigrants (CCI), other ecumenical groups, and the federal government to sponsor, host, and provide ad hoc support to refuge-seekers and immigrants. These partnerships gave them insight into the needs of the community they were serving and connected them with the services available to meet these needs.

The ROC's activities took a sudden and significant turn on May 5, 2005, when the First Unitarian Congregation of Ottawa invited them to a meeting to discuss an uncommon request. Pierre and Margo Gauthier represented the ROC at this meeting, which was attended by a number of representatives from the First Unitarian congregation, including their social worker, Joan Auden. Joan told them of a woman in Ottawa, Sarah, who needed the community's help.

Prior to her life in Canada, Sarah had been a school teacher in Côte d'Ivoire, teaching underprivileged, migrant children from neighbouring Burkina Faso. She had also established a two-acre vegetable farming cooperative to financially empower Burkinabé mothers and help them pay for their children's school supplies. Then in 2000, politicized ethnic violence erupted in Côte d'Ivoire following the country's presidential and parliamentary elections over the contested nationality of the Ivorian opposition leader, who was widely believed to be of Burkinabé origin (Human Rights Watch 2001). In January 2001, an attempted coup against the government sparked additional sectarian violence, religious persecution, and xenophobia toward foreign nationals in Côte d'Ivoire, including harassment by state security forces and extortion by vigilante groups. Additionally, police and paramilitary forces perpetrated manifold human rights abuses such as arbitrary detention, sexual assault, and torture of civilians.

Amidst the political unrest, Sarah's connection to her Burkinabé students led the government to suspect her of being an opposition supporter and her vegetable cooperative of being an anti-government plot. As punishment, Sarah was assaulted by soldiers one night. The morning after, she fled her village to the city of Abidjan, where she received medical treatment for her injuries. At the time, all she could think to do was escape further violence. Her family and friends in Abidjan raised money to purchase an airline ticket to the United States, so that she could travel to join her husband who was there on a student visa. She entered the United States with a visa later that year.

Shortly after her arrival in the United States, Sarah and her husband travelled to Canada seeking refugee status. Their joint hearing was conducted in English, at her husband's insistence, though she would have been more comfortable in French due to her francophone background. She explained her story to the Immigration and Refugee Board of Canada (IRB) member—the sole adjudicator of her claim—through an interpreter. The member did not find her account credible, nor did he believe that she would be in a precarious position if she returned to Côte d'Ivoire. Her application was denied. Her immigration lawyer at the time advised against appealing to the courts for judicial review of her decision, because he felt that her grounds for appeal were weak.

In the months following the refusal, Sarah and her husband separated. She found a new lawyer, named David Morris, who believed in her case and helped her, in October 2004, to apply to stay in Canada on humanitarian and compassionate (H&C) grounds. Shortly thereafter, she received a deportation order set for June 30, 2005, even though her H&C application had yet to be processed. With very few options left, David Morris referred Sarah to Joan Auden and the First Unitarians in the spring of 2005, knowing that they had just finished supporting another refugee claimant in a similar situation. For eighteen months, the First Unitarian Church had acted as a "sanctuary" to a Bangladeshi refugee claimant under a similar deportation order.

Sanctuary has deep historical roots. In biblical accounts, fugitives from the law could enter into the tabernacle's sanctuary and claim refuge by reaching the altar and grabbing onto its "horns" (1 Kings 1:49–53, 2:28–34). Sanctuary also took place on a bigger scale in cities of refuge when municipalities designated themselves as places where fugitives could not only receive protection from the law but also atone for the deeds for which they were accused (Michels and Blaikie 2009). The Bible records this practice in Joshua 20:1–6: "When he flees to one of these cities, he is to stand in the entrance of the city gate and state his case to the elders of the city." The practice of sanctuary continued in medieval times, when fugitives could seek shelter in sacred places to delay or avoid criminal prosecution (Marshall 2014).

Sanctuary practices have gradually declined with the rise of the modern state system and the secularization of Western societies and their penal systems (Lippert 2005a). In 1623, King James I of England formally abolished the practice, which was later restricted in other parts of Europe (Lippert 2005a). When states provide refugee claimants sanctuary from persecution, they absolve civil society organizations and private citizens from the moral responsibility to do so (Macklin 2021, 33). Yet faith-based communities around the world continued to champion their moral right to provide sanctuary (Pope 1987).

The 1980s marked a surge in sanctuary cases across Canada and the United States. In these years, a large number of refuge-seekers fled war and instability in Central America—instability that was greatly fuelled by American Cold War politics. Faith-based communities grew increasingly concerned for the safety of unsuccessful refugee claimants within their countries being threatened with deportation. The arrival of Central American refugees particularly transformed the "geography of refuge" in Canada (Young 2013, 233). Sanctuary became a means of protecting not "fugitives from the law" but rather "fugitives from injustice" (Marshall 2014, 38). A so-called sanctuary "underground railroad" was established by the refugee-transporting wing of the US sanctuary movement to provide those fleeing violence in Central America with "safe houses" in the United States or safe passage to Canada (Cunningham 2012, 162). Local refugee advocates in Detroit and Windsor also facilitated overground entry at the Canada–US border (Young 2013, 236).

Sanctuary has often proven to be a successful tactic for securing refugee protection in Canada. Sanctuary providers have "interpose[d] themselves as a shield between those they recognize as refugees and a government bent on *refouling* (returning) those refugees" (Macklin 2021, 31). In one of the first documented cases of asylum-seeking through sanctuary in Canada, in December 1983, a twenty-two-year-old Guatemalan man sought refuge in St. Andrew's United Church on the outskirts of Montreal (Lippert 2005b). His time in sanctuary garnered considerable media attention, including a televised press conference hosted by his sanctuary providers to advocate on his behalf by explaining why they feared for his safety if he were returned to Guatemala. The man was eventually granted a stay of deportation.

From 1983 to 2009, faith-based communities across Canada participated in fifty acts of sanctuary involving 288 refugee claimants and their immediate family members (Lippert 2005b, 2009). Sanctuary incidents primarily took place in larger cities like Montreal, Vancouver, Winnipeg, Calgary, Toronto, Ottawa, and Edmonton, though they also took place in port cities and smaller cities close to the US border. Local political authorities as well as church communities provided support for sanctuary in most cases. Rather than seeking to conceal the presence of refugee claimants, communities publicized the stories of those in sanctuary, making it politically difficult for authorities to pursue deportation. Amazingly, sanctuary successfully delayed deportation and led to permanent legal status in all cases, except those in which refuge-seekers voluntarily left sanctuary to go underground or cooperated in their deportation. Interestingly, no sanctuary providers were charged for violating Canadian law.

For Ottawa's First Unitarians, sanctuary had produced similar results. So convinced of the merits of their Bangladeshi friend's case and the danger that awaited him if he were returned to his country of origin, the church offered him sanctuary in July 2003—an offer which he accepted. There he remained until December 2004, when he was finally granted a temporary resident permit by then-Immigration Minister Judy Sgro (CBC 2004).

When Joan Auden and the First Unitarians evaluated Sarah's claim, they felt that she, like their Bangladeshi friend, had been unjustly refused. They knew that she needed protection and that sanctuary could be the solution. However, they had just finished providing sanctuary a few months prior and were burned out from the volunteer commitment and financial costs of doing so. They began to look to other churches in the Ottawa community that might be able to take on her case. Since Sarah was Catholic, they felt St. Joe's might be best suited for her situation. They proposed this to Pierre and Margo, explaining that they believed that sanctuary would delay her deportation and allow her to remain in Canada as she awaited a decision on her H&C application. The First Unitarians also offered to help defray Sarah's outstanding legal fees.

Having received the request, Pierre and Margo convened the ROC on May 9, 2005, to share Sarah's story with the rest of the members. The other members present—Michèle, Louise, Yvette, Marg, and Irene—listened carefully and discussed what role, if any, the ROC was prepared to play in helping Sarah. There were many questions about sanctuary's legality. Two Committee members were civil servants who worried about taking a position that could be understood as opposition to federal government policy. Additionally, they wondered how they could provide adequate support with just a little over half-a-dozen members. Yet it was undeniable to them that Sarah's case was urgent and worthy. Michèle Gascon, who was the ROC's chair at the time, remembers that after that meeting she reflected and thought, "I'm 45. Look at the life I've had. Look at where I was born. Why not?" Similarly, Pierre remembers: "We felt duty-bound in conscience to help a refugee claimant who was ordered deported without a complete, fair, and just hearing" (CIMM 2006a). After this deliberation, Michèle moved for the ROC to take on a leadership role in providing Sarah sanctuary, and the motion was passed.

Still, the ROC did their best to pursue any other means of resolution. On May 24, Irene Kellow met with Sarah, her lawyer, David Morris, and an immigration official for a final review of Sarah's case. David asked to be allowed to submit new evidence in regard to Sarah's assault, which he thought put her request for reconsideration in a new light. The official refused to even glance at it and simply responded that Sarah would be picked up on June 30 to be taken to the airport. Irene remembers it was a chilling moment.

Sarah, Irene, Pierre, and David met again on June 13 at David's office to assess if any other options remained. They resolved that sanctuary was likely the only resort and spoke with Sarah to confirm her willingness to enter into sanctuary, even if there was a possibility that the outcome could be negative. They explained that if she were to enter into sanctuary, she would have to do so under two conditions: first, that she not speak to anyone without approval from the ROC, and second, that she not leave the building. Pierre reasoned that these conditions would help ROC members control media portrayals of the sanctuary case and prevent Sarah from being taken into custody.

The next day, the ROC met with the Parish Council to seek their approval for supporting Sarah in sanctuary. After some discussion, St. Joe's Parish Council expressed their support but concluded that it would not be feasible for Sarah to remain in sanctuary in St. Joe's itself. The Council explained that the building was unsuitable and too porous, due to the number of people accessing the building for the Women's Centre, the Supper Table, and other Parish ministries. Such conditions would not afford Sarah adequate privacy and protection. Instead, the Council recommended consulting the Oblate Fathers at Paroisse Sacré-Coeur, the francophone parish located just across the street from St. Joe's on Laurier Avenue, to see if they would be willing to shelter Sarah on their premises. Sarah had attended Sacré-Coeur as a parishioner and had been baptized there, so the partnership seemed only natural.

Pierre met with Father Patry, pastor of Sacré-Coeur, shortly thereafter. He explained Sarah's situation and asked if the parish community could assist in protecting her by providing her sanctuary. The council agreed and the two churches established a partnership whereby Sacré-Coeur would provide sanctuary under their roof, while the ROC would take responsibility for and coordinate other necessary services like meals; medical, social and legal assistance; advocacy; publicity; fundraising; volunteer assistance; and other logistics. Laura Guillemette, who became Sacré-Coeur's sanctuary liaison with the ROC, remembers that some Sacré-Coeur parishioners had concerns about what it would mean to have someone in sanctuary in their building: "At the beginning it was hard for some parishioners to hear that ... it would take space away, it takes the room away, it takes some of the liberties away that some people think they should have." But these concerns were minimal.

With these essentials sorted, the ROC voted to establish three subcommittees—sanctuary, accompaniment, and media—to tackle the different dimensions of sanctuary, from mundane to more serious tasks. Pierre led volunteers for the sanctuary subcommittee, concentrating on addressing Sarah's basic needs, as well as communicating with her lawyer and other immigration officials involved in her case. Louise led the accompaniment subcommittee, made up of parishioners from both St. Joe's and Sacré-Coeur, with the aim of tending to Sarah's personal needs and accompanying her during what would likely be a very isolating experience. Volunteers provided distraction, some through entertainment, others by the development of skills. And finally, the media and political lobby subcommittee, also led by

Pierre due to his interest and skill in navigating the intricacies of political action, was responsible for coaching Sarah through media interviews, sharing her story publicly, and persuading government officials to take up her case.

* * *

Thus began what Louise later called "the greatest challenge of [the ROC's] existence." On June 27, 2005, Sarah entered into sanctuary, three days before her scheduled removal from Canada. On the eve of what would have been her removal, Pierre called the Canada Border Services Agency to inform them that Sarah would not be reporting to the airport the next day because she was officially in church sanctuary. At Sacré-Coeur, Sarah was given a meeting room with an adjoining kitchenette where she could prepare her own food, though St. Joe's Women's Centre and St. Joe's Supper Table prepared daily meals for her. In terms of coordinating logistics, sheltering Sarah was a twenty-four-hour-per-day commitment in keeping with the practice of providing protection. For security reasons, Sarah was to be accompanied by volunteers around the clock to ensure that she was never alone. In the event that law enforcement attempted to forcibly remove her from the church, the volunteer present was not to interfere but to alert the media to get immediate publicity. To make this work, Louise enlisted a huge number of volunteers from both St. Joe's, Sacré-Coeur, and the local community. Night shifts were covered by the priests who lived in the rectory.

On August 24, 2005, the sanctuary committee posted a notice in the Parish bulletin informing parishioners about Sarah's background story and the support she would require from the parish community over the coming months. The notice read: "Serving and working with this person in sanctuary will be an education on the refugee issues in Canada for all of us. As we strive to live our mission statement, it will challenge us as a community of faith to share solidarity with a woman in need of friendship and support. It will take all of us to help this one person" (ROC Archives 2005).

Many parishioners responded, eager to assist. Louise wrote volunteer guidelines, including an information sheet posted at Sacré-Coeur instructing volunteers how to respond if an attempt to remove Sarah was made during their shift.

Under these circumstances, Sarah was resourceful and spent her days improving existing skills and gaining new ones. Dorothy

Collins gave her a sewing machine and she and Deborah Dorner taught her how to sew her own garments. Pat Barr tutored her in English for several hours a week to increase her reading and writing proficiency. Together, Sarah and Maureen Monette made "AIDS angels," hand-stitched dolls to raise funds for children's AIDS relief in Sub-Saharan Africa. Even though her own financial situation was precarious, she gave back to others, illustrating not only her compassion for others but also her resilience and her determination to make the best of her situation.

Prior to entering into sanctuary, Sarah had also rented and operated a kiosk at Hazeldean Mall in Kanata. In the summer, she sold sunglasses and, in the winter, hats and toques. Since Sarah was determined to run her business from sanctuary if she could, Pierre arranged a meeting with the shopping centre's management team to explain Sarah's predicament. The management team agreed to keep her kiosk open and promised not to increase her rent in her absence. With these accommodations, and with access to a computer, she continued to operate her business from Sacré-Coeur, while a host of volunteers from the two parishes and community, coordinated by Pierre Jean-Louis, took shifts to help run her kiosk.

ROC members arranged for a post-traumatic stress counsellor from the University of Ottawa Health Centre to work with Sarah. They also made arrangements for the director of the University of Ottawa Health Centre to make house calls pro bono in case Sarah required immediate medical attention.

The media and political lobby subcommittee was busy strategizing ways to get the government to reconsider Sarah's refugee claim. As early as August, the ROC began receiving requests from the media for interviews with Sarah. She was initially reluctant to have her story aired publicly, feeling that that would require her to offer up too many of the private details of her life. The subcommittee knew that this was true but eventually convinced her that her story was the only thing that could win over public opinion and help to put pressure on the government. As a result of Sarah's change of heart, interviews and stories appeared in numerous local and regional newspapers over the summer.

In an early conversation with Sarah, Pierre made an important discovery. She mentioned that a doctor had examined her the morning after her assault in Côte d'Ivoire. The doctor had even written a medical report exempting her from teaching for three weeks due to the trauma she had suffered from the assault. Pierre was surprised to learn that her first lawyer had not realized that this report could serve as crucial evidence in support of her claim. Pierre discussed the importance of getting a copy of the report. He asked whether she had any family or friends in Côte d'Ivoire to whom she could reach out. Sarah undertook to contact her friends for help in getting the report. This process took her several months and she paid five to six hundred dollars in processing and transportation fees, but by September 2005, three months into her time in sanctuary, she received a copy of the detailed report. The doctor had described the wounds Sarah had sustained in such detail that a Canadian doctor could easily corroborate them if she was willing to submit to a medical examination to validate the report. Sarah's lawyer submitted a brief to the IRB stating that they had obtained new evidence that had not been presented at her initial hearing.

At the time, Peter Showler, former chair of the IRB, was advising a number of sanctuary providers across Ottawa. When he heard about Sarah's case, Showler read the decision-maker's negative refugee decision and read the transcript of the hearing. He recognized immediately that the IRB member who had refused the claim lacked the judicial skills and the self-awareness necessary to adjudicate the case: "He was actually a very nice person but he could not see past his own opinions and presuppositions, and that is lethal for a decision-maker who is supposed to objectively analyze the claim and listen to the testimony with an open mind."

Showler wrote an analysis pointing out a number of legal errors in the reasons, as well as factual conclusions that were not justified by the evidence. Many of the adjudicator's inferences in regard to Sarah's assault appeared, to Showler, to be inconsistent with the IRB's guidelines on gender claims. He offered the opinion that the decision was fundamentally flawed and merited a rehearing.

Meanwhile, to raise awareness about Sarah's situation and to increase pressure on the government, on November 23, 2005, Joe Gunn, Pierre, and media subcommittee members organized a bilingual, interfaith prayer vigil called "Free [Sarah]" at Sacré-Coeur. The vigil was followed by a press conference and a candlelight walk to Parliament Hill. Around four hundred participants—from St. Joe's, Sacré-Coeur, and the First Unitarian Church, plus local refugee rights supporters—came out on that cold November night to show their support for Sarah. Joe recalls: "The cops [blocked] off the streets and were driving slowly with us.... I had organized that we had somebody from the Conservative,

NDP, and the Bloc Québecois [parties]. ... We had them all speak. I [walked] around with a megaphone and I [forget] what we were yelling. 'Free [Sarah]' or something, and the people were responding."

Institutional leadership from St. Joe's, Sacré-Coeur, and the Catholic Archdiocese of Ottawa also got publicly involved to lend their support. Ottawa Archbishop Marcel Gervais personally visited Sarah in early and mid-January 2006. In a thank you letter to Archbishop Gervais, Pierre exclaimed, "Your public support for [Sarah] presents a strong and symbolic message of what we hope our faith communities can become—prophetic servants of those who are vulnerable and marginalized" (ROC Archives 2006).

Still, months passed with little indication of when Sarah's confinement would end. As was the case for the majority of sanctuary cases in Canadian history, however, the government made no discernable attempts to retrieve Sarah from sanctuary. In an interview, Sarah recounted, "The hardest thing about it was being inside, seeing the sunshine and all the seasons coming and going. You feel like life is flying and you can't do anything." During what was surely a lonely, isolating winter for Sarah, she and her friends passed the time playing cards and sharing personal stories. They often discussed what Sarah wanted to do once she was out of sanctuary, such as sharing a meal with her friends in their home and taking their dogs for a walk down the river. Volunteers also brought her home-cooked dinners and desserts to add variety to her menu.

On December 19, despite the far from ordinary circumstances, accompaniment volunteers hosted a Christmas potluck at Sacré-Coeur to celebrate the holidays with Sarah and help boost her morale six months into her time in sanctuary. Under such unusual circumstances, one volunteer described Sarah as "a remarkable spirit," noting that she remained full of life in spite of her situation (ROC Archives 2005). Laura Guillemette, Sacré-Coeur's sanctuary coordinator, said of her, "[Sarah] was a very organized and determined woman...she rallied her friends and some good people around her.... She took care of the business from sanctuary and we just basically made sure that we had volunteers to support her in all her activities."

* * *

A major turning point came six months after her entry into sanctuary when Sarah and members of the sanctuary committee met with Mauril

Bélanger, Member of Parliament for Ottawa-Vanier in December 2005. After learning that Sarah's hearing had been conducted in English despite the fact that she was a francophone, Bélanger was outraged. He told the sanctuary committee that if they were unable to bring this discrepancy to light, then he would. This was the kind of intervention for which the ROC had been hoping from the start.

Bélanger's office filed a complaint with the Office of the Commissioner of Official Languages. Bélanger reported: "I have listened to the tapes of the hearing and found a number of places where the meaning was slightly distorted between the answers [Sarah] gave and the translation" (ROC Archives 2006). Within a week, an investigator from the Commission was appointed to review Sarah's case. On February 2, 2006, the investigator met with Sarah to assess her language abilities. Sarah's supporters were hopeful that this big break would lead to a new hearing. Still, they did not hear anything for another few months.

Sanctuary was a much larger financial commitment than the ROC was used to undertaking. In particular, the costs of Sarah's legal fees and applications totalled approximately five thousand dollars, graciously reduced from nine thousand dollars by Sarah's lawyer. The sanctuary committee set a fundraising goal of ten thousand dollars to cover these and other expenses. Louise and other ROC members canvassed religious communities for donations and raised two thousand dollars. One parishioner made an anonymous donation of five hundred dollars. The First Unitarian Congregation contributed fifteen hundred dollars to cover a portion of the legal fees Sarah incurred.

Then on April 1, 2006, nine months into her confinement, the ROC held a benefit concert entitled "Waiting for Justice," to raise money for Sarah's sanctuary fund. The idea to organize a benefit concert came from St. Joe's parishioner and choir member Marc Coderre back in December, and Maureen Monette helped coordinate the concert planning. The concert featured folk singer-songwriter Tom Lips and choirs from St. Joe's, Sacré-Coeur, and the First Unitarian Congregation. Fortunately, the sanctuary committee raised $8,469.60 after expenses from the benefit concert plus the other donations—enough to cover most of Sarah's sanctuary costs.

Still awaiting news from the Official Languages Commission, Sarah celebrated her birthday in sanctuary in April. Volunteers organized a potluck and presented her with two giant cards signed by audience members from the "Waiting for Justice" benefit concert.

Mauril Bélanger even sent her a beautiful bouquet of flowers for the occasion. Sarah was very touched by everyone's kindness and thoughtfulness.

Then on April 13, 2006, the investigator from the Official Languages Commission came once more to Sacré-Coeur for a follow-up interview with Sarah. He informed the sanctuary committee that a preliminary report would be made available in early May. While they waited for the report, Pierre met with Stockwell Day, Minister of Public Safety and Emergency Preparedness, on April 27, 2006. He requested that the arrest warrant and removal order against Sarah be lifted. The Minister asked for more information so that his staff could review the case. The media and political lobby subcommittee was encouraged by Minister Day's response and hoped that his involvement would encourage a dialogue between Citizenship and Immigration Canada and the Canada Border Services Agency regarding Sarah's situation.

Before any other avenues could be pursued, however, in mid-May, the Office of the Commissioner of Official Languages released its report. The investigator concluded that Sarah's language rights had, indeed, been violated and that her case could be reopened on that basis. Instead, Citizenship and Immigration opted to grant her a temporary resident permit, just as the refugee claimant from Bangladesh at the First Unitarian Church had received when he left sanctuary. This kind of permit allows otherwise inadmissible foreign nationals to remain in Canada for a designated period of time.

On June 20, 2006, Sarah walked out of the church on a bright and sunny day, hand in hand with Pierre and Mauril Bélanger. She was greeted by chants of "Sarah! Sarah!" from supporters who had lined the streets around Sacré-Coeur to celebrate her long-awaited freedom. After a long, challenging year, her time in sanctuary had finally come to an end. Pierre and Margo accompanied Sarah to the Canada Border Services Agency's office, where she was officially released from her deportation warrant. A celebratory luncheon was held later that afternoon at Gerry & Isobel's Café Boutique in Old Chelsea, Quebec.

* * *

In total, Sarah remained in sanctuary for 358 days. The ROC's courageous decision to spearhead a sanctuary case in partnership with

Sacré-Coeur and with support from the First Unitarian Congregation resulted in Sarah gaining legal status in Canada. Sarah transitioned out of sanctuary with help from members of the sanctuary committee; she moved into Carty House. By January 2007, Sarah was granted permanent residence, and in November 2013, she officially became a Canadian citizen.

The achievement of Sarah's freedom required significant intervention—from immigration experts such as Peter Showler and parliamentarians like Mauril Bélanger, as well as from faith communities who took the leap of providing sanctuary for nearly a year. Sociologist Randy Lippert writes that "positive outcomes of a political tactic such as sanctuary have to be tempered with recognition of the psychological and physical toll on individual migrants and migrant families confined to buildings not designed for habitation for months on end" (2005a, 398).

Churches are not intended to be living spaces, at least not for extended periods of time. And Sarah experienced this firsthand. However, ROC members remember that despite not being able to leave Sacré-Coeur, Sarah maintained a positive outlook and inspired others with her good spirits. Even though Sarah did not "even have the liberty to step outside to feel the sun, the wind, or even the rain drops gently falling," Michèle Gascon remembers Sarah being "remarkably calm and keenly interested in visitors and their views" (ROC Archives 2006). Michèle added, "[Sarah] is an amazing lady. She has brought people together and she keeps her spirit up. It must be her deep faith. If it was me, I don't know how I could survive. Bravo [Sarah]."

Regarding the late Mauril Bélanger, who advocated for her and took her case to the Official Languages Commission, Sarah said:

> Having listened to me, Mr. Bélanger was touched by my cause and decided to support the [Refugee Outreach] Committee in search of a solution. A staunch defender of Francophonie, he came up with the idea of having my documents reviewed by a linguistic team of the Office of Official Languages. The team effectively discovered linguistic and legal flaws in how my file had been processed. That was for me the opportunity to witness Mauril's ability to bring together francophone experts to fight for the cause of the French language. … It is thanks to Mauril Bélanger's determination and dedication, as he supported the

> Refugee [Outreach] Committee, and to the support of his wife
> Catherine, that I finally could fulfill my dream of many years,
> that of settling in Canada. (Small 2018, 36–37)

The ROC's decision to provide sanctuary to Sarah in 2005 was not typical of their prior activities. They had opposed certain government actions in the past, but never as overtly as this. For instance, in 1991, the ROC partnered with St. Luke's Lutheran Church to gather three hundred signatures during a Sunday Mass to petition the Ministers of Employment and Immigration to cancel the deportation of a Nicaraguan family of refugee claimants. Sadly, the petition was unsuccessful, and the family ended up going into hiding to avoid deportation. Over the years, the ROC also joined a number of networks and advocacy groups, including in 1995, the Coalition in Ottawa for Refugees (COR), a network of faith-based and community organizations engaged in private sponsorship in Ottawa. Then in 1996, the ROC became a member of the Canadian Council for Refugees (CCR), Canada's leading non-profit organization advocating for the rights and protections of refugees. Membership in the CCR allowed the ROC to network and exchange information with like-minded groups. It also enabled them to participate in national dialogues on refugee rights.

Sanctuary was quite a different form of action, however; it pulled the ROC into what many considered active civil disobedience. This kind of activity, at the edge of legality, was somewhat uncomfortable for some members of the ROC and Sacré-Coeur. Some members worried about their involvement in actions that, although ethically sound, seemed to contravene Canadian law. In fact, some members of the ROC abstained from participating in the sanctuary case (for example, a member who did not wish to compromise their employment in the federal government). One member recalls that it put her in a difficult position to be involved in something that was considered, by some, as illegal, since she had two children living in the United States. She worried that, if charged with a crime or an offence, it might make it impossible for her to visit them. Instead of helping directly with Sarah, therefore, she continued doing peripheral work for the ROC's other initiatives.

Members who directly participated in providing Sarah sanctuary and advocating for her permanent stay in Canada had different views on the legality of their actions. Some rejected any notion that their actions were illegal by continually maintaining that what they were doing was a last resort, after all existing legal options failed to protect her. In the meeting with MP Stockwell Day, Pierre argued that they were providing Sarah sanctuary "as an exceptional action" after many years of collaborating with the government. Pierre was of the view that the optics of intervention in sanctuary were not in the government's favour—an assumption that other ROC members, though, felt was too optimistic. In the event, not all members were comfortable with providing sanctuary, and some opted to associate only with the ROC's other hosting and sponsorship activities during the span of Sarah's time in sanctuary.

Critics of sanctuary and its legality often cite section 131 of the *Immigration and Refugee Protection Act* (IRPA), which states, "Every person who knowingly … aids or abets … a person to contravene section … 124, or who counsels a person to do so, commits an offence and is liable to the same penalty as that person." In this view, offering sanctuary to unsuccessful refugee claimants assists them in contravening section 124 by failing to comply with their removal order. As Sean Rehaag (2009) outlines, inasmuch as faith-based communities aid, abet, and counsel migrants to enter into sanctuary, they may be liable to the same punishment, in this case two years in jail and a fine of fifty thousand dollars.[1] Moreover, there are no laws in Canada precluding law enforcement from entering places of worship to arrest people in sanctuary.

There is some debate about whether providing sanctuary is an act of civil disobedience. Kimberley Brownlee (2017) defines civil disobedience as a "public, non-violent and conscientious breach of law undertaken with the aim of bringing about a change in laws or government policies." Civil disobedience falls between legal protest, on the one hand, and revolutionary action, on the other. Those who engage in civil disobedience are willing to accept the legal consequences of their actions. Audrey Macklin (2021, 36) explains that because civil disobedience involves conscientious, or intentional, law-breaking, "[t]echnically sanctuary qualifies as civil disobedience only if providers correctly believe that sheltering a person under a deportation order violates criminal or immigration law."

---

1   See Rehaag (2009) for the legal definitions of aiding, abetting, and counselling and how these apply to sanctuary providers.

Even if sanctuary does not violate the law, it certainly defies state authority (Macklin 2021, 36). In 2004, Judy Sgro, the Minister of Citizenship and Immigration under Paul Martin's Liberal government, called on churches to abandon the practice of sanctuary, saying it contravened the rule of law. The Minister also implied that it was a matter of safety for Canadians, by saying: "[Sanctuary is] a very difficult issue to deal with and, frankly, if we start using the churches as the back door to enter Canada, we're going to have huge problems. The protection of our country and of Canadians has to be the No. 1 concern. And people shouldn't be allowed to hide anywhere" (Michels and Blaikie 2009, 1).

Advocates for sanctuary contend that its (il)legality is not so black and white, however. Sanctuary supporters across Canada countered the Minister's fear-inducing rhetoric by pointing out that churches only intervened when the Canadian government itself was in danger of violating international law as it relates to refugees (Rehaag 2009, 46).

According to Michels and Blaikie (2009) and Macklin (2021), contemporary sanctuary providers act as an extralegal review body of sorts, carefully screening failed refugee claimants before offering them sanctuary. In many ways, this screening process resembles the official refugee determination system, since providers of sanctuary usually include lawyers, who assess claimants' fears of persecution, examine supporting documentation, and evaluate the legal basis for claimants' admissibility according to the principles of refugee law to which Canada is bound (Rehaag 2009). In a sense, sanctuary relocates sovereignty "by taking it out of the hands of a government-sanctioned official and moving it into [the] moral space of the 'ordinary' citizen" (Cunningham 2012, 172). Sanctuary is a complicated undertaking due to the competing yet intersecting legal systems at play—domestic, international, and canonical—albeit to varying degrees (Rehaag 2009, 51). Sanctuary providers find themselves in a paradoxical position against the government: "in order to advance the solidaristic goal of creating the conditions for agency and autonomy of refugees, [they] become implicated in restricting the liberty they seek to secure" (Macklin 2021, 42). For these reasons, not all who request sanctuary receive it.

Many refugee advocates, including both lawyers and religious leaders, have argued against labelling sanctuary an act of civil disobedience, preferring to frame it instead as a form of *civil initiative*.

Refugee lawyer Kristin Marshall (2014, 38) argues that changes to Canadian refugee legislation stand in such stark contrast to Canada's international obligations that sanctuary providers undertake "a civil initiative to uphold Canada's obligations" rather than acting in contempt of Canadian law. Similarly, Richard Free of the Presbyterian Church has stated that sanctuary is a means to ensure the protection of life and that churches step in, not to operate above the law, but instead "to hold Canadian law to its highest legal obligation" (Westhead 2012). Reverend Darryl Gray of Montreal's Union United Church has also explained that "moral institutions cannot obey laws that are unjust" and that church leaders are "prepared to accept the penalty for this civil initiative" (Michels and Blaikie 2009, 2). To this end, faith-based communities regard themselves as allied with the government in ensuring refugee protection.

Additionally, although success has frequently been the outcome, it is not guaranteed. At two points in Canada's history, church sanctuary has been breached. The first instance occurred in March of 2004 when officers entered Saint-Pierre United Church in Quebec City and forcibly removed an Algerian man slated for deportation to the United States (CBC 2005). In reaction, protests were held in Vancouver, Toronto, Ottawa, Montreal, and Quebec City to dispute the man's arrest and his forced removal from sanctuary. Unfortunately, these public demonstrations did not prevent his deportation. In the end, the man was sent to the United States, where his initial claim for asylum had been rejected. Luckily, the man was able to file an appeal with the American Board of Immigration Appeals (BIA), and fifteen months later, the decision was overturned and he was granted refugee status in the United States. Though his time in sanctuary may not be counted as a success, those who gave him refuge were somewhat vindicated when the BIA confirmed the legal argument made by the church that had provided him sanctuary—that he was a legitimate refugee claimant (Rehaag 2009). The man returned to Canada in 2009 to reunite with his wife who had been living in Montreal, and he soon after applied for permanent resident status.

The second instance in which sanctuary was breached in Canada demonstrates another of the strong disincentives for providing sanctuary. Sanctuary comes with a great deal of publicity and exposure for both the refuge-seekers involved and the faith communities that support them. In February 2007, police entered St. Michael's Anglican church in Vancouver to arrest an Iranian man who had been living in sanctuary for nearly three years. His supporters firmly believed that he would be tortured due to his political leanings if he were returned to Iran. Additionally, his mother had received refugee status in Canada by presenting nearly identical fears of persecution. After his arrest, his supporters were quick to draw media attention with a major article published in the *Globe and Mail* raising awareness about the man's situation (Armstrong 2007). Within two days, he was granted permanent residence on H&C grounds (Rehaag 2009).

* * *

As these stories and the situation of the ROC demonstrate, providing sanctuary is no simple task. Sanctuary requires extraordinary sacrifice from all parties involved. So why do faith communities do it? In Canada, refugee advocates justified many sanctuary cases because of systemic flaws in the refugee determination system. The system, then and now, is well known for its deficiencies and weaknesses. Refugee claimants often lack access to sound legal representation, interpreters, and documentary evidence of their claim (CCR 2012; Showler 2006). IRB members have frequently made decisions based on mistaken assumptions about credibility, human behaviour, or memory (Evans Cameron 2010; Cohen 2001). They may be unprepared, prejudiced, or careless and may re-traumatize refugee claimants in their manner of questioning (CCR 2012; LaViolette 2014).

Compounding the system's flaws, in 2001, Parliament passed the IRPA and made a series of controversial changes to Canadian refugee law. Most notably, the IRPA reduced the number of members (judges) adjudicating each refugee claim from two to one. The government claimed the reduction would increase processing efficiency. Refugee advocates were concerned, however, that this would disadvantage claimants, since dual-member decisions were viewed as an important safety valve to protect refuge-seekers from the variability in member's decisions (Macklin 2009, 146–147). Previously, under the dual-member system, disagreements that arose due to the overall merits of a case were resolved in favour of the claimant. Regardless, the government proceeded with this change.

In exchange, the federal government promised to create a long-awaited appeal process for refugee claimants. The provision was even included in the newly passed IRPA (sections 110, 111, and 171). The Refugee Appeal Division (RAD) would allow decisions to be reviewed if a claimant felt the deciding member had made a mistake. In consultations about this new law, the IRB's then-chair Peter Showler testified: "It is true that claimants will no longer enjoy the benefit of the doubt currently accorded them with two-member panels. ... However, any perceived disadvantage is more than offset by the creation of the Refugee Appeal Division ... where all refused claimants and the minister have the right to appeal the decision" (CIMM 2007a).

Still, when the Act came into force in 2002, the RAD was not implemented. Successive immigration ministers in different governments continued to delay the RAD's implementation, citing a variety of reasons. They pointed to its operating costs and its possible interference with the large number of claims already waiting to be heard by the IRB (Clark 2002).

Unsatisfied by the government's excuses, a wide range of advocates put out calls to immediately operationalize the RAD. The CCR argued that "the implementation of the Act without the right of appeal subverts the will of Parliament and undermines the democratic process" (CIMM 2006b). Members of Parliament had agreed to the reduction in judges for each case and had done so believing that an appeal process would serve as a check. The United Nations High Commissioner for Refugees (UNHCR) addressed the issue in a letter to the Minister of Citizenship and Immigration in 2002, stating: "UNHCR considers an appeal procedure to be a fundamental, necessary part of any refugee status determination process" (CCR, n.d.). Amnesty International called the delay in implementing the RAD "enormously frustrating," and NDP immigration critic Olivia Chow (MP for Trinity-Spadina) criticized the federal immigration department and its minister for "showing contempt for the House of Commons" (CIMM 2007b). Even Parliament's multi-partisan Standing Committee on Citizenship and Immigration unanimously passed a resolution in 2004 calling for the Minister to implement the RAD.

And, of course, the delays and excuses were unacceptable to the refugee claimants who lived with the consequences and the injustices of non-implementation of the RAD. Their only legal recourse, to avoid deportation, was to apply to the Federal Court of Canada for judicial review, a process whereby an individual can challenge a decision made by an administrative tribunal by bringing it before a federal judge for review of fact and law. However, they must first apply for permission (or leave) to do so from a federal judge and such applications are successful in only a small number of cases. Of the 6,939 refugee cases submitted to the Federal Court in 2005, the year of the ROC's sanctuary case, only 1,034, or 14.9 percent, were granted judicial review (CIMM 2007a). RAD advocates argued that judicial review was not a sufficient safeguard for failed refugee claimants, pointing out that federal judges lacked expertise in refugee law, whereas an RAD could provide both this expertise and develop a body of precedents over time to make decisions less arbitrary.

Some claimants sought to delay or prevent their departure by applying for a Pre-Removal Risk Assessment (PRRA).[2] A PRRA requires a refugee claimant to submit a letter explaining the risk they would face if they were to leave Canada, while providing evidentiary documents to support this claim. PRRA applications allow refugee claimants to raise new evidence but not to argue that the initial decision was wrong. If the PRRA is accepted, in most instances the applicant becomes a protected person who cannot be deported from Canada despite not having refugee status. Yet, in 2005, when Sarah faced deportation, the chances of success under either of these options were slim: only three percent of PRRA decisions were positive (IRCC 2008).

Other refugee claimants sought to remain in Canada by applying for permanent residence on H&C grounds. Such applications can be made when an individual seeks an exemption to one or more requirements in the IRPA. However, such decisions are highly discretionary, since deciding officers must be convinced of the hardship or difficulties that would result from being refused such as health considerations, family violence considerations, consequences of the separation of relatives, and any unique or exceptional circumstances meriting relief (Government of Canada 2020a). When approved, H&C applications lead to permanent residence status. Yet H&C applications offered, then and now, limited immediate protection since applicants under removal orders must still depart on their designated removal day, whether or not a decision has been rendered on their application. Processing times and backlogs for H&C applications were often egregious, as they still are now; in 2019, 4,681 permanent residents were admitted to Canada based on H&C considerations, but

---

2   Changes in law in 2012 now prohibit a person whose refugee claim has been rejected from seeking a PRRA if less than twelve months has elapsed since the claim's refusal. Therefore, only those whose deportation has been delayed long enough for circumstances to change in their country of return have access to this option (IRCC 2012a).

approximately 18,500 applications remained in the processing queue for in-Canada H&C cases (Government of Canada 2020a; Government of Canada 2020b).

With so few avenues to avoid being returned to their countries of persecution, it is no wonder that many who were offered sanctuary were willing to sacrifice their freedom of movement for a chance to avoid deportation. Since governments were unlikely to sanction the use of police force to breach sanctuary and since most documented cases of sanctuary were successful in delaying or entirely preventing deportation, it was seen by many faith-based communities as a legitimate act of *civil initiative* to provide hope to refuge-seekers and ultimately to protect them from being sent back.

Sarah's time in sanctuary caused the ROC and parishioners to confront the injustices inherent in Canada's refugee determination system first-hand. As the ROC saw it, their advocacy for Sarah was neither the beginning nor the end of their fight for the right to seek refuge in Canada, since refugee claimants still did not have access to an adequate appeal process. In years following, the platform the ROC gained through their involvement in sanctuary allowed them to push for reform in the refugee determination system, specifically in advocating for the establishment of an RAD at the IRB. Chapter 3 will explore the ROC's advocacy on this front in the years following Sarah's release from sanctuary.

Sarah's and the ROC's success through sanctuary is a testament to the extraordinary actions ordinary people are willing to take to advocate for the right to seek refuge. After Sarah's release, a celebratory Parish bulletin concluded: "Of course, any account of the good work that resulted in freedom for [Sarah] will leave out the names of many persons of great goodwill who helped along the way" (ROC Archives 2006). Many of Sarah's advocates were neither politicians nor legal professionals nor political strategists. Rather, they were dedicated volunteers seeking to protect her from the persecution she would likely have faced if Canada had followed through on the decision to deport her. As Pierre put it, "The lesson we learned from [Sarah's] case: if the cause is just, never give up the fight."

Chapter 3 Timeline

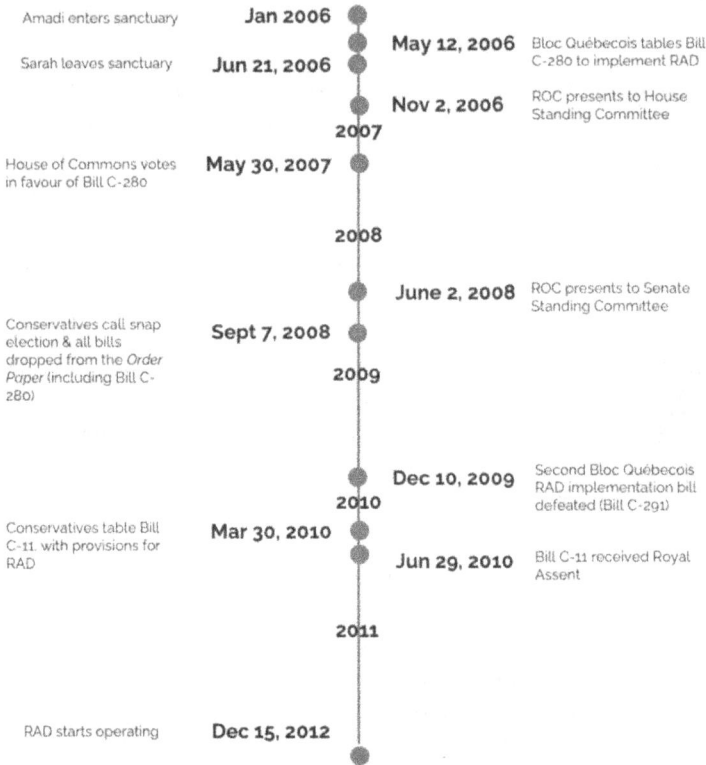

Amadi enters sanctuary | **Jan 2006**

May 12, 2006 | Bloc Québecois tables Bill C-280 to implement RAD

Sarah leaves sanctuary | **Jun 21, 2006**

Nov 2, 2006 | ROC presents to House Standing Committee

2007

House of Commons votes in favour of Bill C-280 | **May 30, 2007**

2008

June 2, 2008 | ROC presents to Senate Standing Committee

Conservatives call snap election & all bills dropped from the *Order Paper* (including Bill C-280) | **Sept 7, 2008**

2009

Dec 10, 2009 | Second Bloc Québecois RAD implementation bill defeated (Bill C-291)

2010

Conservatives table Bill C-11, with provisions for RAD | **Mar 30, 2010**

Jun 29, 2010 | Bill C-11 received Royal Assent

2011

RAD starts operating | **Dec 15, 2012**

CHAPTER 3

Post-Sanctuary Advocacy

The members of the Refugee Outreach Committee (ROC) sighed a big breath of relief after Sarah's sanctuary case came to a successful end on June 21, 2006. Lauchlin Chisholm, a member of the ROC's media and political lobby subcommittee, captured Sarah's supporters' elation over her long-awaited freedom when she was finally able to "walk outside unimpeded and feel the grass and look freely at the expanse of the sky" after living inside Sacré-Cœur's building just shy of one year (ROC Archives 2006). "To paraphrase," Lauchlin wrote, "she was free at last, free at last."

In providing Sarah sanctuary, the ROC and St. Joe's parishioners experienced first-hand the results of the failings of the refugee determination system. Their involvement in the case solidified their view that refugee claimants should have the right to appeal negative decisions if they felt their claim had been wrongly decided. Like Sarah, thousands of refuge-seekers were being placed at risk each year by a system that allowed a single, fallible member at the Immigration and Refugee Board (IRB) to decide whether they merited asylum—without any recourse to an appeal.[1]

---

1 As explained in Chapter 2, the changes introduced to refugee law under the *Immigration and Refugee Protection Act* (IRPA) in 2001 reduced the number of IRB members making decisions on refugee claims from two to one, while making provisions for a Refugee Appeal Division (RAD). The RAD was, however, never implemented.

The ROC's role in sanctuary linked them to an ecumenical network of faith communities in Ottawa who agreed that establishing a Refugee Appeal Division (RAD) was vital to Canada's refugee determination system. In the summer of 2005, while Sarah was in sanctuary, the ROC joined the First Unitarian Congregation in collecting signatures for a petition to the House of Commons calling for the RAD's implementation. The petition amassed 240 signatures from Sacré-Coeur, 223 signatures from St. Joe's Parish, 170 signatures from the First Unitarian Church, and 25 signatures from St. Paul's Eastern United Church, located near the University of Ottawa campus.

The petition was officially presented to members of the House of Commons at the protest on Parliament Hill after the "Free [Sarah]" vigil on November 23, 2005. It was tabled in the House by staunch RAD advocate, Bloc Québécois Member of Parliament Meili Faille, on November 28, 2005. Faille expressed her agreement with the petitioners' requests in a speech to her colleagues that same day:

> In the interests of efficiency, a specialized appeal division is a much better use of scarce resources than recourse to the Federal Court, which is not at all specialized in refugee matters. In the interests of consistency of law, an appeal division deciding on the merits of the case is the only body able to ensure better interpretation of jurisprudence. In the interests of justice, as in matters of criminal law, the right to appeal to a higher tribunal is essential for the proper administration of justice. (House of Commons 2005)

In the absence of an RAD, the ROC continued to offer moral and financial support for other sanctuary cases in Ottawa. In January 2006, the All Saints Lutheran Church in the west end of the city took a young Ethiopian man, Amadi, into sanctuary. Amadi had originally arrived in Montréal in the summer of 2001 to attend an international human rights conference, where he learned that government informers from back home were looking for him. Amadi fled to Ottawa, where he filed his refugee claim and began attending All Saints Lutheran Church. Unfortunately, his refugee claim was denied, because the deciding member did not find his fears credible. That same year, he faced deportation to his home country, where he feared he would be tortured or killed due to his belonging to a persecuted ethnic group, as well as because of his family's affiliation with an opposition political party.

Sarah and Amadi's sanctuary cases overlapped with the election of a Conservative minority government in February 2006, formed under the leadership of Stephen Harper. In regard to refugee claimants, the government began to develop what some viewed as a "discourse of distrust," portraying them as persons trying to "fool" or "take advantage" of the Canadian immigration and social welfare systems (Carver 2016, 210). The Harper government would go on to repeatedly claim that the Canadian refugee protection regime was "too generous" and that a more rights-restrictive and discretionary approach was needed to prevent those who did not actually require protection from obtaining "undeserved economic, political, and/or social benefits in Canada" (Anderson and Soennecken 2018, 292).

The injustices perpetrated by the lack of an appeal process and restrictive immigration policies were obvious not only to the ROC but to refugee advocates across Canada. Action was needed to challenge the security-infused rhetoric put forward by the Harper government.

On May 12, 2006, a few weeks prior to Sarah's release from sanctuary, Nicole Demers—a Member of Parliament representing the Bloc Québécois and her constituency of Laval—introduced Private Member's Bill C-280. This bill called for the coming into force of provisions made in the *Immigration and Refugee Protection Act* (IRPA) for an appeal division which, until that point, had not been implemented (sections 110, 111, and 171). These sections of the Act authorized a refugee claimant or the Minister of Citizenship and Immigration to appeal a decision to allow or reject the person's claim for refugee status. In the appeal process, the RAD would then take one of three actions: confirm the initial determination; substitute the decision with a determination that, in its opinion, should have been made instead; or refer the case to the IRB for redetermination. On the day that she tabled the bill, MP Demers rose in the House of Commons to state: "Mr. Speaker, for four years now, the federal government has been stubbornly delaying the creation of the appeal division under the *Immigration and Refugee Protection Act*. It is time that the government respected the legislation and implemented the appeal division, which is why I am introducing this bill" (House of Commons 2006).

In Canada, when a bill is tabled in the House of Commons, it goes through three readings. The first reading allows members to understand what issues the bill addresses. The second reading opens the bill's scope to debate. If a bill passes the vote cast after its second reading, then generally it is assigned to a committee for further review, which involves calling on experts and people affected by the bill to provide their respective insights and analyses. The committee then produces a report and can also make amendments to the bill before sending both back to the House. The House debates the bill again and proceeds to the third and final reading, after which the chamber votes on the bill and any amendments. The bill is then passed on to the Senate to follow a very similar procedure and vote (House of Commons, n.d.).

Although some bills move through the various stages relatively quickly, others, as we will see with Bill C-280, advance at an excruciatingly slow pace. Though it was tabled in May 2006, debate on the matter was deferred until January 2007. Still, MP Demers' bill became a rallying point for many refugee advocates, including the ROC.

The ROC was determined to stay involved in efforts to advocate for refugee rights. Then-ROC Chair Michèle Gascon accompanied Sarah to visit Amadi in sanctuary several times as an act of solidarity. Sarah and Amadi shared the same lawyer, and the success of Sarah's case provided the Lutheran Church's sanctuary committee with great hope for Amadi's chances of remaining in Canada. Yet, ROC members could see that there would be many people like Sarah and Amadi in the future if something did not change. They believed the system had failed both, despite their clear need for refugee protection. Notwithstanding the merits of Amadi's case, no legal mechanisms could prevent his deportation.[2] The ROC felt that sanctuary would not have been necessary for Sarah, Amadi, or others in their position had there been an adequate appeal process in place.

After a brief rest following Sarah's release from sanctuary at the end of June 2006, in September the ROC began to strategize how they could be involved in lobbying the government for the RAD's implementation (through Bill C-280 or by other means). The ROC organized a RAD subcommittee, led by Pierre Gauthier and joined by Lauchlin Chisholm, who had both demonstrated their knack for political manoeuvring during Sarah's year in sanctuary. The RAD subcommittee also collaborated with a number of formidable allies in the community. Peter Showler, former IRB chair and University of Ottawa law professor, had advised a number of sanctuary committees across the city and brought a wealth of knowledge about the IRB's

2   In the end, Amadi remained in sanctuary for twenty-one months and was granted permanent residence in October 2007 (CBC 2007).

day-to-day functioning and the intricacies of refugee determination. Joe Gunn, who had previously organized the walk to Parliament on behalf of Sarah in sanctuary, had worked throughout his career in the ecumenical humanitarian networks across Ottawa and Canada. When asked how he got involved with RAD advocacy, Joe responded with a chuckle: "Bad luck. Pierre twists your arm and makes you come out to meetings."

The ROC's RAD subcommittee began looking for ways to collaborate with other like-minded groups and to continue expressing its concerns about the lack of an appeal process. Around this time, St. Joe's began receiving invitations to speak to parliamentary committees about their experience with Sarah. As Pierre explains, the ROC was well known in Ottawa and beyond because of their participation in sanctuary: "The politicians saw how effective we were in getting our case through. And without us bragging or describing our process, they understood because they saw us hit the right notes and the right keys, [and get results]." He added, "They respected that. So that's why they invited us." Peter Showler emphasized just how unique the contribution of faith communities really was at the time:

> The Canadian Council for Refugees, all the NGOs, and secular agencies had been presenting a strong argument for an appeal process but sanctuary gave the churches a unique entry point into the dialogue and the process. They were the only institution in Canada offering an alternative form of protection. Most churches did not grant sanctuary casually. They knew that their refugees had not received fair treatment and spoke from a position of strong moral authority.

Pierre and the RAD subcommittee members enthusiastically agreed both to speak before government officials and to present a brief to the House Standing Committee on Citizenship and Immigration once the House resumed later that fall. The brief was prepared by Pierre, Joe, and Lauchlin, with the assistance of Ottawa's First Unitarian Church and the All Saints Lutheran Church. Lauchlin's writing experience as a former journalist and public relations professional, as well as the editor of St. Joe's monthly newsletter *St. Joseph's Spirit*, was a particular asset.

The House of Commons Standing Committee on Citizenship and Immigration convened on November 2, 2006, to discuss refugee issues, especially as they related to sanctuary.[3] Invited to speak on the issue were Pierre Gauthier (from St. Joe's ROC), Heather MacDonald (from the United Church of Canada), Mary Jo Leddy (from Romero House and the Sanctuary Coalition of Southern Ontario), Stephen Allan (from the Presbyterian Church in Canada), Phil Nagy (representing the First Unitarian Church), and Gordon Walt (representing the All Saints Lutheran Church).

In succession, each of these presenters laid out the systematic and personal ways in which the refugee determination system had failed the refugee claimants they knew (CIMM 2006a). Mary Jo Leddy spoke in powerful opposition to the oft repeated argument that other options—such as Pre-Removal Risk Assessments, application for humanitarian and compassionate (H&C) consideration, and judicial review—already amounted to an appeal for refugee claimants, saying that the current system offered a "labyrinth of partial appeals." She argued that a RAD "would be far less costly and less expensive than the inefficient morass that swamps the refugee determination process." Heather McDonald from the United Church of Canada argued that churches had stepped in to provide sanctuary not in defiance of the law but in "respect for the law and the justice it demands of it." All Saints Lutheran Church's Gordon Walt echoed this sentiment, saying, "We are naturally very angry and upset about being put in this position, but as people of faith, we really do not have any other choice."

Like the speakers before and after him, Pierre shared a short but powerful message. He reminded the Standing Committee of the role small faith-based organizations and communities like St. Joe's ROC usually play: "[T]o carry out simple acts of everyday kindness. For refugees in need, we help find living quarters, furniture, warm clothes, and jobs." He explained how in 2005, when the ROC learned of the ways the immigration system had so unjustly treated Sarah, they felt duty-bound in conscience to go beyond their usual role. Pierre emphasized, "Churches have been put in the invidious position of offering sanctuary only because the refugee determination system is not working properly. Clearly, when a valid refugee claimant has to

3   Members of the Standing Committee at the time included Norman Doyle (CPC), Blair Wilson (Lib.), Andrew Telegdi (Lib.), Meili Faille (BQ), Bill Siksay (NDP), Ed Komarnicki (CPC), Barry Devolin (CPC), Nicole Demers (BQ; acting on behalf of Johanne Deschamps), Rahim Jaffer (CPC), Gurbax Malhi (Lib.; acting on behalf of Raymonde Folco), and Joe Preston (CPC; acting on behalf of Nina Grewal) (CIMM 2006c).

turn to a church for help, there is a problem with the system." He openly wondered about the hundreds, if not thousands, of refugee claimants who have likely been turned away from Canada because they—like Sarah from St. Joe's or Amadi from the All Saints Lutheran Church—did not have the opportunity to fully present their case to the IRB.

Pierre then enumerated the recommendations of the ROC to the Standing Committee. First and foremost, they asked the government to implement the RAD as stipulated by the IRPA. Second, they called for an increase in the number of members hearing cases at the IRB in order to solve the backlog. Third, they encouraged the government to provide greater guidance to the IRB regarding refugee claimants' language rights, noting that in Sarah's experience, translation and interpretation services during hearings had ultimately been a decisive issue. Finally, Pierre denounced the lack of institutional accountability the ROC witnessed while Sarah was in sanctuary, stating, "[F]or the entire year we cared for a refugee claimant in sanctuary, the bureaucracy avoided talking to us."

Following their presentations, Pierre and others were briefly questioned by members of the Standing Committee—two of whom had previously been refugees themselves (Liberal MP Andrew Telegdi, originally from Hungary, and Conservative MP Rahim Jaffer, originally from Uganda). Opinions on the Standing Committee varied, as they always do, but questions seemed sincere. The Standing Committee chair, Conservative MP Norman Doyle, finished by stating that their words and recommendations would be included in a report, and the Committee would sit and consider what they had been told before making a recommendation. He finished, however, by saying, "I don't believe that I can say on behalf of the Committee whether we will make that recommendation [to implement the RAD], but I can tell you that most of the Committee members from whom I've heard on this matter are very sympathetic to it." Bloc Québécois MPs Meili Faille and Nicole Demers reminded the members of the Standing Committee that they would have a chance to discuss this further as Bill C-280 passed through the House.

* * *

Though the results of their presentation to the Standing Committee on Citizenship and Immigration were not immediate, the ROC continued to seek avenues to publicize their demand for a refugee appeal process. In fall 2006, Maureen Monette from St. Joe's Parish and members of the First Unitarian Church's sanctuary committee teamed up to organize a multi-faith advocacy event called "Refugee Dilemma." This event, held at St. Joe's on November 15, 2006, was the first performance of a play written by Peter Showler. The play tapped into his prior experience as a member of the Refugee Protection Division at the IRB and dramatized a chapter from his book *Refugee Sandwich*, which consisted of thirteen fictional short stories examining challenges that confronted both refugee claimants and the Board members assigned to their cases within Canada's refugee determination system (Showler 2006).

The play, entitled *Excluding Manuel*, told the story of a refugee hearing for a man accused of participating in torture in his home country before coming to Canada to seek asylum. The role of Manuel was played by a former Guatemalan refugee, and the rest of the cast were refugee lawyers from Ottawa's Legal Aid offices, including Michael Bossin, Ann Scholberg, Laurie Jo, and Chantal Tie. Bossin and Scholberg portrayed the two member judges making a decision on the hearing, Jo played the dutiful clerk, and Tie narrated.

The evening was very well attended. An audience of about two to three hundred people filled more than half the cavernous church. Many in the audience were members of St. Joe's congregation recruited by the ROC, but there was an equal number from the legal and academic communities due to advertising by the Refugee Forum at the University of Ottawa and the Refugee Lawyers' Committee of the Ottawa Bar Association. The play portrayed a number of systemic injustices within Canada's refugee determination system, including the biases or indifference of judges when making life altering decisions; poor interpretation services; the lack of access to legal representation; and other procedural inequalities. That evening, the community raised $1,120 (after expenses) to donate to the All Saints Lutheran Church to help cover the sanctuary costs for Amadi, the Ethiopian man in their care. Peter Showler went on to present *Excluding Manuel* nearly twenty times over the next few years in Ottawa and Toronto to continue raising money and awareness for both sanctuary cases and the need for systemic reform.

In the new year, the ROC continued to pressure the government to establish the RAD as mandated in Bill C-280. A number of new members joined the RAD subcommittee, including Megan Reid, a law student at the University of Ottawa and former member of the media and political lobby subcommittee, and Lisa Barnet, a law student and member of the ROC since September 2006.

When the House of Commons resumed after the Christmas holidays on January 29, 2007, Bloc Québécois MP Meili Faille moved, in the House of Commons and during Private Members' Business, that Bill C-280 be read for a second time and referred to a committee for assessment. This gave MP Nicole Demers (who had introduced the bill back in May 2006) another chance to argue for the implementation of the RAD. In her speech, she lauded the sanctuary efforts of St. Joe's ROC and other Ottawa faith-based groups by name. Yet she argued that "justice should be rendered without the necessity to call on the intervention of strong and well-organized pressure groups," saying, "A proper appeal process for refugee claimants ought to have been put in place as soon as the Immigration and Refugee Protection Act enacted in 2002 took effect. This is one of the significant changes required to ensure that asylum seekers are treated fairly and equitably" (House of Commons 2007a).

After her speech, a number of MPs spoke in solidarity. Liberal MP Omar Alghabra declared that he would support the bill and called out the Conservative government for "exhibiting very little compassion and understanding to the real humanitarian issues of immigrants and refugees," despite the fact that the Liberal government had also not implemented the RAD during their years in office. The NDP's Bill Siksay stood to say that his party "strongly supported" the bill, while stating that it should not be necessary, considering the RAD provisions already made in the IRPA. He also pointed out the unusual nature of the bill: "I think it is a very unusual piece of legislation, though, in that to have to debate ... a bill to implement legislation that has already been passed in this place is a very unbelievable situation" (House of Commons 2007a). On the other side of the debate, Conservative MPs argued that the bill was unnecessary, considering the other options for redress available to unsuccessful refugee claimants.

Unfortunately, the motion to move to a second reading was not voted on that day but, instead, deferred to March 2, 2007, clearing bureaucratic hurdles at a snail's pace, as is often the case with legislation introduced by members privately rather than by their party. In the meantime, the ROC's RAD subcommittee held an important meeting on February 28, 2007. Special guests Peter Showler, Mauril Bélanger (and his executive assistant), and author and former law clerk of the House of Commons Joe Maingot attended the meeting to help to launch the group and refine the objectives they hoped to achieve (ROC Archives 2007). During this meeting, the RAD subcommittee agreed that they should continue to pressure the federal government to expedite review of Bill C-280. They also addressed a letter to then-Minister of Citizenship and Immigration, Diane Findley, to express their heartfelt concern for the many deserving refugee claimants facing deportation from Canada without recourse to an appeal and a fair hearing, again citing Sarah as an example of a refuge-seeker whom the system repeatedly failed. The letter affirmed the ROC's call to implement the RAD and declared their solidarity with other refugee advocates, including the Canadian Council for Refugees (CCR) and KAIROS, an active interfaith group of churches in Canada—and other groups working on behalf of refugee claimants (ROC Archives 2007).

On March 2, 2007, when the House of Commons finally held its second debate on Bill C-280 during Private Members' Business, voices from each party joined in, mostly reiterating their prior points and positions. Finally, and though the vote was deferred once more until March 21, the House passed the motion to have Bill C-280 referred to the committee stage for further evaluation. The vote was 172 in favour to 126 against (House of Commons 2007b).

A few weeks later, the ROC's RAD Advocacy Group received a reply to their letter from Minister Findley's office. While acknowledging the need for improvement, the response skirted around the system's major problems. The Minister's office argued that even without the RAD in place, Canada's refugee determination system was one of the fairest and most generous in the world. The letter reiterated that the implementation of the RAD would add months to an already lengthy refugee determination process. It stressed the great importance of getting decisions right the first time and added that recourse was already available in the form of Pre-Removal Risk Assessment (PRRA) or H&C applications. The Minister's representative concluded by explaining that "...the government is committed to improving the system in order to ensure that it delivers its decisions more efficiently. It is equally important to ensure that decisions lead to concrete results—permanent residence for those in need of protection and timely removal for those found not to need international protection" (ROC Archives 2007).

On the heels of this frustrating response, Bill C-280 was read for a third time and the ROC received the news they had been hoping for. On May 30, 2007, the House of Commons voted in favour of Bill C-280, with 151 for and 119 against (House of Commons 2007c). Bloc Québécois,

Liberal, and NDP MPs voted in favour of the bill, along with one Independent MP, while all Conservative MPs and two Liberal MPs voted against.

That day, Pierre sent out a congratulatory email to the rest of the ROC upon learning the good news: "I thought I should relay the good news I received this afternoon…. Bill C-280 received approval by the House of Commons," and then noted, "Now it must go to the Senate and then hopefully get royal assent in the fall" (ROC Archives 2007). Reflecting on the ROC's advocacy efforts during the sanctuary case and beyond, Pierre added, "I like to think that our efforts advocating for the implementation of the RAD contributed in some way to this bill passing." Unfortunately, their celebrations came too early; this would not be the end of the struggle for RAD implementation.

* * *

As Parliament readied for its return that September, Louise emailed NDP MP Paul Dewar—son of former Ottawa mayor and NDP MP Marion Dewar—asking for a status update on Bill C-280. Dewar responded within a few days, informing her that the Senate had read the bill for the first time the same day it was passed in the House of Commons. It was then debated by the Senate on June 12 and June 19, 2007. Once the bill passed its second reading, it would be sent to a Senate committee for review.

Clearly supportive of the ROC's call to implement the RAD, MP Dewar expressed his frustration over the refusal of successive immigration ministers to do so. "This is not an expensive proposition," wrote Dewar, "it is a paper screening process." He believed that the lack of a merit and fact-based appeal process drove many failed refugee claimants underground and led others to seek sanctuary in churches, as the ROC knew very well. "Let me take this opportunity to commend you and the rest of the Refugee Outreach Committee at St. Joe's Parish for your efforts to make Canada a more socially just society," he concluded. It heartened ROC members to see Bill C-280 making its way through the Senate, but the RAD subcommittee's work was far from over.

On October 24, 2007, members of the RAD Advocacy Group participated in an event called "Rally for Refugee Rights: Flaws in Canada's Refugee System" hosted by the Interfaith Refugee Network of Ottawa at the First Unitarian Church. The event was attended by politicians, representatives from different faith communities, and representatives from unions and human rights organizations. Among the attendees were Paul Dewar, the Canadian Labour Congress's National Director for Human Rights, the Senior Director of the Jewish Federation of Ottawa, and the Eastern Ontario Director of the Canadian Auto Workers' Union. Father Kelly, St. Joe's pastor since 2002, and Pierre spoke on behalf of the Parish at the event. Margo and Louise also attended. Father Kelly recounted that parishioners at St. Joe's "learned that by praying for and working with refugees, we ourselves are assisted in becoming what we really want to become as caring members of the human family" (ROC Archives 2007). Father Kelly and Pierre's comments were later featured in an overseas broadcast by Radio Canada International.

At the ROC retreat in November 2007, the Committee reflected on their advocacy efforts to date and their plans for 2008. They agreed to continue lobbying government officials on Bill C-280 through the RAD subcommittee. They also turned their focus to sensitize the parish community about the need for an RAD through articles in the parish newsletter and bulletin, workshops and events. Additionally, the RAD subcommittee remained committed to providing advice and information about sanctuary and sponsorship to interested parties.

On March 4, 2008, Bill C-280 passed its second reading in the Senate and was sent to the Senate Standing Committee on Human Rights. Though refugee advocates insisted that the Committee need not spend a great deal of time reviewing the bill (since it called for an appeal division that the Senate had already approved when the IRPA legislation passed in 2001), it still proceeded to plod on ever so slowly through the different stages of review (CCR 2008).

* * *

As they awaited movement in the Senate, ROC members appeared once again before the House Standing Committee on Citizenship and Immigration the following week, this time to discuss Bill C-50, the *Budget Implementation Act*, introduced by the Conservative Finance Minister, whose provisions ostensibly intended to reduce a backlog of cases in the Canadian immigration system. The bill, which had been introduced in February of that year, proposed amendments to the IRPA including discretionary powers for the Immigration Minister to introduce special instructions to process different categories of citizenship and immigration applications. Should the bill pass, it would allow the Minister to limit the number of applications to be processed in any year and to dispose of applications that were not processed. The bill also proposed the elimination of overseas applications for H&C consideration (Parliament of Canada, Bill C-50 87.3[3] and 87.3[4]). Critics argued that Bill C-50 favoured efficiency at the expense of fairness (Russo 2008). These concerns were echoed by immigration and refugee advocates who appeared before the Standing Committee.

RAD subcommittee member Lisa Barnet accompanied Pierre to the May 14, 2008, meeting. Representatives from the Islamic Humanitarian Service and Inter-Cultural Neighbourhood Social Services also spoke. In his address to the Standing Committee, Pierre raised doubts about whether the changes proposed in Bill C-50 would result in clearing the immigration application backlog (CIMM 2008). The ROC also felt that it was politically and procedurally inappropriate to include changes to immigration law in a budgetary bill. Any amendment to the IRPA should rather be debated and studied on its own merits in separate legislation. Pierre concluded with a plea for fair, open, and transparent immigration processes.

Their views were shared by the Senate Standing Committee on National Finance, who after reviewing the bill, made observations in June 2008 that major amendments to the IRPA belonged in a standalone bill that could properly address the backlog of applications in the immigration system, rather than in a bill pertaining to budgetary matters (NFFN 2008). The Senate's agreement was a small victory for groups like the ROC, who dedicated countless hours of unpaid volunteer advocacy to lobby the government on behalf of refuge-seekers and immigrants. Unfortunately, Senate committees' observations have no procedural significance and are neither debated nor voted on by the Senate. Therefore, Bill C-50 was passed as drafted and the proposed changes to the IRPA were adopted when the bill received Royal Assent on June 18. All in all, it took this bill just a little over five months to pass, while Bill C-280 languished in the legislature some thirteen months after being tabled.

* * *

Still, the ROC had good reason to hope that Bill C-280 would ultimately be successful, after having succeeded in the House of Commons. On June 2, 2008, during the Senate's review of Bill C-280,

Pierre, Lisa Barnet, and ROC member Jan Raska were again asked to appear in Parliament, this time before the Senate Standing Committee on Human Rights. Again, they presented alongside representatives from the First Unitarian Congregation. As they had previously done, they shared an overview of their churches' involvement in sanctuary and, therefore, the need for an RAD. Pierre incited Standing Committee members to think of those not lucky enough to find a champion to take up their cause, who are then "summarily removed to their fate in the uncertain and troubled land from which they fled" (RIDR 2008).

Jan Raska acknowledged the Canadian government's generosity for accepting and sponsoring hundreds of refugees every year, but addressed the need for systemic change, asking the Standing Committee to "please assist [the ROC] in making our system better and allowing, even if only on a limited basis, for the opportunity to introduce a mechanism for correcting errors in the system" by passing Bill C-280.

When the Senate Committee rendered their report a few weeks later on June 18, Bill C-280 was passed on division, meaning with a clear majority in favour, and with amendments (Senate of Canada 2008a). The suggested amendments were that the effective date of implementation of the bill should be delayed by one year in order to allow the IRB time to coordinate and train personnel. The Standing Committee also asked that the bill clarify who would be eligible to appeal to the RAD once it came into effect. As drafted, the bill allowed for every failed refugee claimant since the passage of the original bill in 2001 to submit an appeal. The Senate warned that this would cause the RAD to start off with a backlog of up to 40,000 potential appellants (Senate of Canada 2008b). As such, they proposed an amendment that would only allow refugee claimants to file an appeal if they were still awaiting a decision at the time the bill passed into law.

When the Senate passes a bill with amendments, the bill must be returned and passed again through the House of Commons. However, before the House could vote on the Senate's amendments, Parliament adjourned for the summer on June 20, 2008. Again, celebration of the passage of Bill C-280—for refugees, the ROC, and other advocates—was delayed.

* * *

More than sixteen months after being tabled, after being passed once by both the House and the Senate, and just as the ROC could see the finish line with Parliament set to return on September 15, 2008, the ROC's high hopes were quashed. In a bid for a majority government, Prime Minister Harper asked the Governor General to dissolve Parliament and on September 7, an election was formally called for October 2008. As a result, all bills, including Bill C-280, were dropped from the *Order Paper*. In a single stroke, the years of work by RAD advocates—inside and outside of Parliament—were wiped out.

The snap election delivered the Conservative Party another minority government, this time with 143 of the 308 seats in the House of Commons (whereas previously they had 124). For Pierre and the ROC's RAD subcommittee this was enough. Worn out from years of advocacy, and somewhat discouraged, they chose to refocus on supporting refuge-seekers in their community and to pass the RAD baton on to other advocates to continue in their stead. On February 5, 2009, Bloc Québécois MP Thierry St-Cyr introduced Bill C-291, which comprised the same text as Bill C-280 on the implementation of the RAD. Thierry invited all members to support the bill, explaining that even though seven years had passed since the RAD was due to come into force and essentially the same bill had already made its way through all stages of the House and the Senate once before, this measure should still be implemented as a matter of justice and to respect the dignity of all those who sought refuge in Canada. Conservative MP Rick Dykstra rebutted, stating that the government's position on Bill C-291 had not changed from that in the 39th Parliament: his government *still* opposed the bill. By December 10, 2009, when the House was presented with the motion to adopt Bill C-291, this time the Conservatives succeeded in narrowly defeating the bill: 142 members voted in favour and 143 voted against (House of Commons 2009). All opposing votes were cast by Conservative MPs, except for one cast by an Independent.

Ironically, only months after the bill's defeat, on March 30, 2010, the same Conservative government introduced Bill C-11, or the *Balanced Refugee Reform Act*, which promised to implement the RAD, but only after a waiting period of two years after receiving Royal Assent. Speaking before the House that day, then-Immigration Minister Jason Kenney announced, "[U]nder the balanced reform announced today, all refugee claimants will have access to a fair process consistent with the Canadian Charter of Rights and Freedoms and with our international and national legal obligations" (House of Commons 2010).

Still, the bill had some significant differences from those presented by prior private members. Bill C-11 was a more comprehensive reform of the refugee determination system as a whole. Bill C-11 was introduced partly in reaction to the arrival of the MV *Ocean Lady*, a migrant vessel carrying seventy-six Sri Lankan Tamil refuge-seekers, off the coast of British Columbia in October 2009. The Tamil refuge-seekers were accused by the government of smuggling drugs, explosives, and weapons into Canada, based on the belief that they were affiliated with the Liberation Tigers of Tamil Eelam, or LTTE, a group deemed a terrorist organization in Canada since April 2006 (Reynolds and Hyndman 2015; Okafor 2020). The bill made provisions to shorten the refugee determination process and authorized civil servants to preside over refugee hearings instead of individuals appointed to office for a fixed term (Library of Parliament 2010). It gave the Immigration Minister power to designate countries whose citizens would be excluded from appealing, as well as to decide the type of evidence that the RAD would review and the conditions under which it would hold hearings. Bill C-11 also barred foreign nationals from applying for H&C consideration if, having made a claim for refugee protection, less than twelve months had passed since a decision was rendered on the claim. Additionally, the bill prohibited failed refugee claimants subject to a removal order from applying for a PRRA in the first twelve months after a claim denial.

The bill was read for a third time and passed unanimously by the House on June 15, 2010, then was read for the first time by the Senate. Unlike the legislation for which the ROC advocated, which took nearly two years to pass through the legislative process and still failed, Bill C-11 speedily progressed through both chambers and received Royal Assent on June 29, only three months after it was introduced. Though the conditions surrounding the RAD's implementation were far from perfect, this was still a victory after so many years of advocacy. Many felt that it was better than having no appeal process at all.

* * *

Bill C-11 gave the IRB two years—until June 29, 2012—to implement the RAD. Even then, the RAD was not formally launched until

December 15, 2012, because of changes brought on by another major immigration reform bill tabled by the Conservative government.

Since the passing of Bill C-11, another migrant vessel, the MV *Sun Sea*, had been intercepted on the west coast, this time carrying 492 Sri Lankan Tamil men, women, and children. The Tamil refuge-seekers were quickly branded by then-Minister of Public Safety Vic Toews as "queue jumpers," "human smugglers," and "terrorists" (Reynolds and Hyndman 2015). Of the 492 refuge-seekers onboard, 443 were detained as part of a strategy to deter other Tamils "who might nurse the ambition of travelling to Canada to seek asylum" (Okafor 2020, 69). The arrival of the MV *Sun Sea* inspired further changes to Canadian immigration legislation in 2012. Bill C-31, the *Protecting Canada's Immigration System Act*, was introduced in February 2012 by the now majority Conservative government (elected in May 2011). Bill C-31 proposed sweeping changes to the refugee determination system, including compressed timelines hindering refugees' ability to obtain sufficient documentation prior to their hearings, and limited access to legal counsel, in an effort to deter "non-genuine" refugees from coming to Canada.

The bill also restricted eligibility to appeal: a decision of the Refugee Protection Division (RPD) rejecting a claim on the grounds that it was not credible would be ineligible for appeal to the RAD. Bill C-31 proceeded through the House and the Senate at lightning speed, passed with 159 in favour and 132 opposed, and received Royal Assent on June 28, 2012—one day before the RAD was set to come into effect. There was little opportunity for refugee advocates to contest the alarming provisions in Bill C-31 before it was passed.

Still, despite eleven years of delay, by December 2012 refugee advocates finally had the RAD they had campaigned for. In its first two years of operation, the RAD received 1,812 appeal applications from refugee claimants. Of these, nearly twenty-nine percent were dismissed on procedural grounds and only about nineteen percent succeeded (Grant and Rehaag 2016). The RAD continues to hear refugee appeals today. In 2018, the RAD finalized 2,774 appeals. Of the appeals submitted by refugee claimants, twenty-two percent were awarded—but nearly three quarters were dismissed (Rehaag 2019). Though the RAD was a significant step in the right direction, the legislative and policy changes in 2012 made access to asylum and to the refugee determination process increasingly difficult. As a likely result, in 2013, the year following the implementation of the RAD,

Canada received fifty percent fewer refugee claimants than it did in 2012, despite a twenty-eight percent rise in asylum claims worldwide (Reynolds and Hyndman 2015). Canada dropped to sixteenth place as a destination for asylum seekers, down from second and third place respectively in 2008 and 2009. There is still a great need to critically examine Canada's refugee determination system.

The history of sanctuary and RAD advocacy clearly demonstrate the central role of faith communities, like St. Joe's ROC, in holding the government accountable in the reformation of refugee law and policy. Their role in providing sanctuary afforded them remarkable credibility in debates on the RAD's implementation. Michael Bossin, a prominent refugee and immigration lawyer in Ottawa who worked with the ROC on a number of occasions, remembers the importance of interventions by faith communities in this fight: "It was one thing for lawyers to go there and say the law was unjust. But it was really important to have their work and advocacy, because [faith communities] had first-hand knowledge."

It is no wonder that the government should prize the extensive first-hand and personal experience gained by faith communities in the settlement sector. St. Joe's ROC members form significant bonds with refuge-seekers as they become friends, share deeply personal experiences, and learn about refuge-seekers' families, faith, hopes, and future plans. They are frequently privy to the intimate details of the events that caused refuge-seekers' displacement and witness their daily efforts to become a part of a new community. This intimate knowledge is valuable from a legal perspective, Michael Bossin says, since refuge-seekers may be more comfortable with their friends in the community than with their lawyers. Volunteers can provide logistical support in gathering evidence and encouragement during times of uncertainty or struggle.

More critically, however, we can see from the testimonies provided above in parliamentary committees that a government that relies on service-providing faith communities to represent the interests of refuge-seekers—instead of listening to refuge-seekers directly, which they too rarely do—inevitably puts faith communities in the settlement sector in an uncomfortable position. Doing so, as Phil Nagy testified to the House of Commons Standing Committee on Citizenship and Immigration, creates a danger that faith communities will become a quasi-official part of the refugee determination process—something that puts these groups in a difficult moral and ethical position. If community members become part of the refugee determination system (i.e., by providing sanctuary) will they be complicit in perpetuating injustices inherent to it?[4] And will playing such a role take scarce resources away from the actual task of settling refugees and refugee claimants?

To this day, volunteer advocates in both faith and secular communities play an important role in championing laws and policies affecting refugee claimants. One might expect that, following the coming into force of the RAD, sanctuary is no longer necessary. Nonetheless, the practice continues, albeit less frequently than it did in the early 2000s. Refugee claimants are still deeply affected by shortcomings at the IRB and in the refugee determination system. Refugee determination is a very tricky business, and the stakes are high (CCR 2012; LaViolette 2014; Hersh 2015; Evans Cameron 2010; Showler 2006). Deciding members must make decisions on the basis of how credible they find claimants' fears of future persecution after listening to their stories and weighing the evidence they submit. Yet members' lack of knowledge of the conditions in claimants' countries of origin or the true nature of their personal trauma can make it difficult for them to assess credibility. Deciding members also have very heavy caseloads, making both hearings and the turnaround time for decisions brief.

Since mistakes are bound to occur under these conditions, the right to appeal is still essential. But it remains limited by certain procedural constraints, including that applicants must currently file a Notice of Appeal within fifteen days of receiving their written decision from the Refugee Protection Division (RPD) and have only thirty days to submit additional evidence that either arose after the rejection of their claim or was not available at the time of their hearing (Grant and Rehaag 2016). Successfully pulling together the necessary documentation within such a limited time typically requires the assistance of expensive legal counsel.

Given the restrictions on the appeals process, there have been several sanctuary cases in Canada since the establishment of the RAD in 2012. In October 2013, a Salvadoran sought sanctuary at Walnut Grove Lutheran Church in Langley, British Columbia. The man and his wife arrived in Canada as refugee claimants in 1997. In 2000, they

---

4   Refer to Chapter 3, p. 39 for a broader discussion on the danger of allowing faith communities to become quasi-official actors in the refugee determination system.

were denied refugee status because the federal government deemed El Salvador a safe country. Four years later, they were approved for permanent residency following a positive H&C application; however, their permanent resident status was never finalized. Then, in 2010, an immigration officer concluded that the man was inadmissible to Canada due to his alleged participation in a political liberation movement during the Salvadoran Civil War in the 1980s and 1990s (Ritchie 2013). He once again applied for H&C, but his claim was denied due to the "terrorist" label attached to the political movement he was alleged to be a part of and, hence, to him. Facing deportation, he sought sanctuary after an arrest warrant was issued in his name by the Canada Border Services Agency in October 2013. In the end, the man remained in sanctuary for two years and finally gained freedom in December 2015 after the newly appointed Minister of Immigration, Refugees and Citizenship, John McCallum, overturned his deportation order on H&C grounds.

In the years following their RAD advocacy, the ROC has continued to witness the ongoing deficiencies of Canada's refugee determination system. In 2014, they also received another request for sanctuary (which we will touch on in Chapter 4). Yet, after reviewing the facts of the case, the ROC recognized that it could not take on the huge responsibility of providing sanctuary for a second time. The ROC's decision not to offer sanctuary illustrates the limits of relying on non-state actors to correct injustices in the refugee determination system, as Pierre and other refugee advocates expressed to Parliament on more than one occasion. The support and advocacy that sanctuary requires from its providers is constant and taxing. Its success largely depends on the long-term dedication and commitment of volunteers and supporters—which cannot always be relied on. Chapter 4 recounts the ROC's post-RAD experiences and demonstrates both the limits of volunteer participation in times of exhaustion and its extraordinary capacity in times of perceived crisis, such as during Canada's Syrian Refugee Resettlement Initiative.

Decline and Resurgence:
The Syrian Initiative

The Refugee Outreach Committee's (ROC's) advocacy for a Refugee Appeal Division (RAD) ended when the 2008 snap election prevented a final vote on the amended Bill C-280. In the wake of the massive efforts that had begun with Sarah's sanctuary case more than three years earlier, ROC members were naturally worn out and increasingly aware of their limitations as a volunteer organization.

Though the ROC had nine active members from 2007 to 2009, six of them had been on the ROC for many years: Louise Lalonde, Margo and Pierre Gauthier, Irene Kellow, Michèle Gascon, and Yvette Lynch. The first four had joined the ROC in the early 1990s, meaning that they had been volunteering for over fifteen years. These six core members were beginning to burn out, which caused a few of them to step away from the ROC. In mid-2009, Louise decided it was time to take a break from the ROC for the first time in the nineteen years since its inception. By the end of 2019, both Michèle Gascon and Yvette Lynch had also left to pursue other projects. Michèle remembers that aside from feeling burned out, she felt it was time for a change.

With Pierre, Margo, and Irene still at the helm, the ROC continued its good work. At this point, the ROC's activities consisted of providing ad hoc support and mentorship to the sponsored refugees and refugee claimants they had assisted in prior years or to others who approached them. Still, it was clear that they urgently needed to recruit new members. This only became more pressing in December 2011 when Margo had to leave the ROC for health reasons.

For several months, the ROC tried to make time to brainstorm ways to recruit new members to whom they could "pass on the experience of [their] senior members." However, this conversation was repeatedly postponed, partially due to more pressing agenda items, such as discussions about refugee claimants' needs or ROC finances, but also because of complications due to legislative and policy changes made by the Harper federal government in 2012 (as discussed in Chapter 3).

In 2012, the federal government made some regulatory and administrative changes to the Private Sponsorship of Refugees Program (PSRP) (CCR 2014; Reynolds and Hyndman 2015). First, it restricted community sponsors to sponsoring only those people who had already been designated as refugees by the United Nations High Commissioner for Refugees (UNHCR) or by a foreign government. This meant that only Sponsorship Agreement Holders (SAHs)—meaning organizations that signed agreements with the federal government permitting them to facilitate sponsorships (the majority of which are faith-based organizations)—could submit applications for people not yet designated as refugees. Second, the federal government imposed caps on the number of new private sponsorship applications that an SAH, like the Catholic Centre for Immigrants (CCI), could submit annually. It also restricted the number of sponsorships referred by visa offices being processed abroad. Third, sponsorship paperwork became more burdensome: whereas sponsor groups had previously had access to the guidance of local officials, now they had to fill out applications themselves, which resulted in many being returned as "incomplete." Other changes included limiting resettled refugees' access to health care and reducing the age of dependent children from twenty-one to eighteen. Additionally, the federal government continued to decrease quotas for Government-Assisted Refugees. Refugee advocates saw this as evidence that the government was increasingly shifting its responsibility to resettle refugees onto private individuals.

In its defence, Harper's government said that these changes would help with long-standing issues of high refusal rates, large application inventories, and long processing times (IRCC 2012b). At the time, the private sponsorship program had a backlog of 29,125 applications. Some Canadian visa offices abroad, or missions, were operating with a backlog in excess of five years (IRCC 2012b). Refusal rates were especially high for sponsor-referred refugees; from 2006 to 2010, the refusal rate was, on average, forty-three percent (Labman 2019, 104). Though refugee advocates had a stake in solving these issues, changes to the PSRP caused them great difficulties in submitting any new applications. For the ROC, this meant that in 2012 their partner, CCI, was given a quota by the government of only four sponsorships. This quota was further limited because the government required CCI to accept sponsorships referred through the Nairobi, Kenya, visa office. The ROC had, however, been hoping to sponsor a refugee who had been referred to them through the Canadian visa office in Cairo, Egypt.

Frustrated by these changes and burned out by the demands of the ROC's work, then-chair Pierre told the ROC that he would be stepping down to act in more of an advisory role by May of 2012. He hoped that someone else would take up the position. However, when the time came, there were no willing candidates. He agreed to remain chair until the June meeting, "on the condition that cookies be provided." By September, the ROC found a temporary solution when they recruited three fresh members. One of these members, Patrick Wells, accepted the role of interim co-chair for the year and Pierre agreed to stay on as treasurer.

This arrangement, however, did not solve the underlying issue, which was that in order to continue providing all the same services for refugee claimants and resettled refugees, the ROC needed members with as much expertise and who could dedicate as much time as Louise, Pierre, Irene, and others had before. Yet no one was in a position to replace these long-serving members.

By March 2013, when Patrick had to step down as co-chair, the Parish's leadership recognized that the ROC, a usually independent outreach ministry, was in trouble. Louise, who was away from the ROC at the time, remembers the Parish was "worried about the survival of the Committee" and chose to ask pastoral associate Mary Murphy to serve as chair. As a pastoral associate and full-time employee, Mary ran a great deal of St. Joe's community outreach and educational programming. Feeling that the ROC was very important to the identity of the Parish, she agreed to help and quickly set out to rejuvenate the Committee.

To rekindle interest in the ROC and to spark the recruitment of new members, Mary organized an evening to celebrate the long-time members of the Committee who had retired. She planned the event for September 12, 2013, as "An Evening of Gratitude and Tribute" to honour the members and their many years of service. In her invitation to the past and current ROC members, as well as the parishioners, Mary wrote:

> This group of passionate and dedicated individuals have reached out to the most vulnerable over these past 25 years with vast amounts of time—expertise in navigating the immigration system and finding help, hauling furniture, sorting through forms and assessing needs, as well as the many hours of building trusted relationships with the most vulnerable, creating friendships, and simply helping people to start again…. As the committee transforms to meet new and developing needs we have a great desire to say 'thank you' to the visionaries of our parish who served in this way. (ROC Archives 2013)

It was a special evening. Many ROC members were reunited and given the opportunity to share their stories. Peter Showler, former Immigration and Refugee Board (IRB) chair, honoured the ROC with an address to thank them for their many years of service to refuge-seekers and their years of activism and advocacy in Ottawa.

Irene retired from the ROC shortly after the celebration. Pierre stayed on but only in an advisory role. In the following months, Mary concentrated on recruiting new members. A few key members joined around this time: Jessica Silva, Robyne Warren, Deborah Dorner, and Radamis Zaky. At Mary's request, Louise also rejoined the ROC to advise and mentor the newer members.

With the ROC's numbers replenished, Mary had to make a decision about who could best serve as group leader. All eyes turned to Jessica Silva, aged twenty-three at the time. Energetic, proactive, and organized, Jessica began attending St. Joe's student mass when she moved to Ottawa in 2013 to pursue her Master's in Public Health. Her master's research was centred on trauma-informed care for refugee women and she had been looking for ways to get involved in refugee work in the community. When she saw the ROC's call for volunteers in the Parish bulletin, she remembers thinking, "This is a sign!"

Jessica remembers that at that time the ROC was very small, saying ruefully: "We kept having to switch rooms [in St. Joe's] because we were so small!" However, Jessica was able to recruit a number of her friends on campus. For the first time in its history, the ROC had a swath of young adults participating. Deborah Dorner remembers "they were a breath of fresh air on the Committee." Still, the ROC was very much in a "reorganizing" phase. Past connections with refuge-seekers through host matches and sponsorships had long since ended or were lost as members had retired from their work with the ROC. In their role as advisors and mentors, Pierre and Louise passed on the expertise and experience gained by the ROC over the years. Pierre delivered training on the ROC's finances. Louise encouraged the group to get involved right away with hosting through the CCI. She reasoned, "[New members] are eager and motivated and expect early hands-on involvement. If that opportunity does not arise their expec-tations are not met, they lose their enthusiasm and drop out. That is why I proposed ... that new members should get involved with host-ing as soon as possible in order not to lose interest and leave." She felt that though she and Pierre could pass on information, nothing could replace first-hand experience. Additionally, their mentoring would take on a greater meaning if it could be applied to real experiences with real people.

Under Jessica's leadership, the ROC focused on sensitizing itself to refugee issues. It also heeded Louise's counsel and prepared to engage in hosting activities. The first step was getting the police checks required for volunteers working with vulnerable people. Members who wished to host were interviewed by CCI and took part in training. But because CCI was in the process of reorganizing the host program, most members were never matched with refuge-seekers. Still keen on sponsoring, an enthusiastic new member, Robyne Warren, helped the ROC form a connection with Capital Rainbow Refuge (CRR), a community dedicated to sponsoring LGBTQ+ refugees, to explore sponsorship possibilities. The ROC also facilitated a co-sponsorship which consisted of co-signing an applica-tion and then arranging with the Parish bookkeeper to hold funds in trust for a Syrian family in the community who wanted to sponsor a Syrian man living in Egypt. The man eventually arrived in Ottawa at the end of 2015.

The biggest challenge for the newly revived ROC came in the summer of 2014 when they received a request from Carty House about a possible sanctuary case. The request was for a woman with five children from Benin, in West Africa. She fled her country after the police had murdered her husband. Still, her refugee claim had been rejected for lack of credibility. Deborah Dorner remembers that the original statements in her claim had been written in haste and without legal assistance. Committee members, including Jessica, Deborah, and Pierre, spent hours and days poring over her case and were convinced that she had a genuine fear of persecution if she were to be deported. Unfortunately, the Parish Council was not able to offer the woman and her children protection in sanctuary. Instead, Committee members went out on a search for other churches willing to offer the woman sanctuary. A number of ROC members were discouraged when these efforts were unsuccessful and, again, a few members left.

* * *

In April of 2015, as the ROC was still stitching itself back together, Jessica's tenure as ROC chair came to an end and she left Ottawa. A number of the student members left at around the same time, having graduated, transferred to other universities, or returned to jobs for the summer. The ROC was once again at risk of near dissolution. In this key moment, Louise sensed that she had to take care not to prevent others from emerging as new leaders. She proposed that she and two newer Committee members, Robyne and Farah, a young Arabic-speaking student, form a leadership team. Robyne agreed but, for personal reasons, Farah could not. At the following meeting, Robyne and Louise offered to serve as co-chairs until the next annual general meeting in a year's time when elections for a chairperson would be held. The ROC readily accepted. Robyne and Louise spent the summer of 2015 clarifying their role as co-chairs and planning a new start to the coming year, not realizing what September would bring.

On September 2, 2015, the shocking image of Syrian toddler Alan Kurdi, drowned and lying on a Turkish shore of the Mediterranean, surfaced on the internet and spread virally. The public soon learned that Alan Kurdi and his family were refugees, displaced by the Syrian war. They had been trying to cross the Mediterranean, as many refuge-seekers have done on their way to claim asylum in Greece, when their dinghy capsized, taking the lives of a dozen Syrian refugees, including Alan, his five-year-old brother, Ghalib, and their mother, Rehanna. After years of widespread governmental and public inertia toward the Syrian War and the huge number of people displaced by it, Alan Kurdi's image sparked Canadian outrage when news came out that members of his extended family had applied for resettlement in Canada but had not been accepted.

This event turned the whole country's attention to the millions of Syrian refuge-seekers who flooded into neighbouring countries and the thousands who attempted the dangerous Mediterranean crossing to seek safety on the shores of Europe. An Angus Reid poll indicated that ninety percent of Canadians had some awareness of the Syrian refugee crisis and sixty-four percent said they were actively following the events (Angus Reid Institute 2015). In a way that prior news coverage had failed to do, the Kurdi family's tragedy inspired renewed activist energy in Canada's response to the plight of Syrian refugees (Siddiqi and Koerber 2020; Adler-Nissen, Andersen, and Hansen 2020; Wallace 2018).[1]

With energized public attention and a Canadian federal election a little more than a month away, the major parties began to focus on refugee resettlement pledges as a key part of their campaigns. In previous years, the Conservative government had promised to resettle 11,300 Syrians between 2013 and 2018; yet in 2015, only 2,500 Syrian refugees had arrived. On September 20, 2015, the Conservative government announced that they would speed up Syrian resettlement by eliminating the requirement for proof of refugee status from the UNHCR and fast-track 10,000 refugees over three years, in addition to the 11,300 they had previously promised to resettle. Canada's New Democratic Party pledged to resettle 46,000 refugees over four years,

---

1   It is important to note here the selectivity of media attention to refugee "crises." Although the Syrian situation at the time of these events was truly urgent, the population of refugees originating from African countries was nearly equivalent to that from Syria. In 2015, UNHCR and the United Nations Relief and Works Agency (UNRWA) calculated that there were approximately 21.3 million refugees worldwide (UNHCR 2015a). Of these, an estimated 4 million (19%) originated from Syria (UNHCR 2015b) and another estimated 4 million (19%) originated from countries on the African continent. More recently, as refugee numbers continue to increase, 6.3 of the recorded 25.9 million (24%) refugees worldwide in 2019 were from African countries, whereas 6.7 (26%) were from Syria (UNHCR 2019a; UNHCR, n.d.). Additionally, the vast majority of African refuge-seekers live in protracted situations, in chronically overcrowded and underfunded camps across Africa. Despite these comparable levels of displacement, since 2015, Canada has resettled 45,875 refugees from the African continent compared to 93,230 from the Middle East (IRCC 2020a). Though a full analysis of the dynamics underlying this discrepancy is outside of the scope of this work, the dynamics of race in Canadian immigration policies are important to consider. For more insights into this discussion, see Walker (2008) and Madokoro (2017, 2018).

while the Liberal Party of Canada pledged to resettle 25,000 Syrian refugees by the end of the year (Globe and Mail 2015).

Many Canadians were unwilling to idly await the results of the election. Across Canada, tens of thousands mobilized to pressure the federal government for increased Syrian refugee resettlement quotas (Macklin et al. 2018). In a manner reminiscent of the 1978 Southeast Asian resettlement initiative, people rallied with neighbours, friends, co-workers, faith communities, and strangers to form Groups of Five. Groups of Five consist of five or more citizens and/or permanent residents who select a refugee and arrange to fund and facilitate their resettlement in Canada. To prepare applications for co-sponsorships, many community groups also turned to SAHs. The ROC co-chair at the time, Robyne, recalls, "[The image of Alan Kurdi] galvanized the world to rescue Syrians and something happened that hadn't happened since the Vietnamese Boat People."

The City of Ottawa was not immune to this galvanization. On October 1, 2015, Mayor Jim Watson and the City Council held a public forum on Syrian refugee resettlement efforts at City Hall. The town hall meeting was attended by over a thousand people, with more than twenty-two community agencies and faith groups represented. With the federal election impending, Mayor Watson said, "We're not sure how many and we're not sure when, but we want to be able to welcome these families properly when they arrive" (City of Ottawa 2015).

Mayor Watson explained that community members could get involved by taking on a private sponsorship and by donating to the cause. He announced that to facilitate these two actions, a grassroots coalition of refugee advocates in Ottawa had come together to form Refugee 613. Under Louisa Taylor's leadership Refugee 613 was a first point of reference for people interested in participating in sponsorship. Refugee 613's aim was to prevent the duplication of efforts and to better communicate information in Ottawa about welcoming refugees, including through sponsorship, hosting, health care provision, housing and other forms of refugee support across the city.[2] Mayor Watson also announced a fundraising initiative, called United for Refugees, to support these efforts.

The forum featured an information fair to introduce the refugee-serving organizations already present in the city and to assist

---

2   Since its inception, Refugee 613's funding has come from federal and provincial government grants, civil society organizations, and private philanthropy.

residents undertaking sponsorships. For instance, nearly forty law-yers from the Refugee Sponsorship Support Program (RSSP), a program run out of the University of Ottawa, were matched with resi-dents wanting to sponsor refugees. The lawyers provided pro bono legal advice and helped sponsoring groups to navigate the applica-tion process (City of Ottawa 2015).

Five ROC members—Louise, Robyne, Radamis Zaky, Connie Goulet, and Deborah Dorner—attended the public forum. When she remembers the event now, Robyne felt she met two kinds of people at the event: "One was the Syrian Canadian who wanted to know how to sponsor their family members and another type wanted to know how to help and/or sponsor the same people."

At St. Joe's, media coverage of Syrian refugees resulted in a surge of Parish volunteers interested in participating in the ROC's work. Between 2014 and 2015, its membership had ranged from six to eight members. By October 2015, Robyne remembers, "All of a sudden we had more people wanting to volunteer than we knew what to do with." To function effectively, the ROC chose to keep its membership to a tight group of twelve. Candidates were interviewed and those selected were expected to go through training provided by the Refugee Sponsorship Training Program (RSTP)—an organization funded by the federal government that supports sponsor groups across Canada.

Robyne and Louise also enlisted a new treasurer. John Weir was a long-standing member of the Parish who had previously helped with Sarah's sanctuary case. He and his wife, Dorothy Collins, visited Sarah frequently, and Dorothy taught her to sew. After seeing the pic-ture of Alan Kurdi in September 2015, John felt he had to do something, and he quickly became very involved in the ROC. He had a knack with computers and accounting—skills that were sorely needed as the ROC navigated growing public interest.

As the grassroots in Ottawa and other cities across Canada organized, on Election Day, October 19, 2015, the Liberal Party of Canada won a majority government. Justin Trudeau was sworn in as Canada's prime minister a few weeks later on November 4. The new federal government reiterated their election promise to expedite the welcome of twenty-five thousand Syrian refugees, modifying their goal by including a mix of both GARs and Privately Sponsored Refugees (PSRs) and extending the deadline to February 2016 (IRCC 2015). This was dubbed the Syrian Refugee Resettlement Initiative (hereafter referred to as the Syrian Initiative).

The end of November 2015 saw a flurry of activity. At the Parish, St. Joe's office manager, Brandon Rushton, noted a surge in phone calls and donations and said in a bulletin addressed to the Parish titled "St. Joe's & the Syrian Refugee Crisis," "I've been very touched by the number of phone calls and emails I've fielded from not only members of the parish, but members of the community who feel an urge to help those in need" (ROC Archives 2005).

The surge in volunteerism and interest in refugee sponsorship was not only felt in the Parish. It was felt across Ottawa. Don Smith,[3] from the Anglican Diocese of Ottawa's Refugee Working Group, recalls that there was only a half-dozen groups in the Anglican Diocese of Ottawa working on private sponsorship in the years and months leading up to the 2015 election. Don recalls how everything changed within a few short months: "It exploded…. We were getting calls every day. By Christmas we had about sixty groups sponsoring through the Diocese."

Across Canada, tens of thousands of people were expressing interest in private sponsorship and forming sponsor groups. In response, Refugee 613 called on long-serving members of the Coalition in Ottawa for Refugees (COR) to host "Sponsorship 101" sessions throughout the city to share the basics of sponsorship with prospective sponsors. The sessions were also to help connect people with others in their area interested in forming sponsorship groups and to connect new sponsors with those with more experience. These sessions were primarily organized by community members: Louisa Taylor (of Refugee 613), Don Smith (from the Anglican Diocese of Ottawa's Refugee Working Group), Norma McCord (of the United Church), and Lisa Hébert (of Capital Rainbow Refuge).

As members of COR and as experienced sponsors, the ROC was also called on to deliver a Sponsorship 101 session. On a rainy evening on December 6, Robyne and Louise presented at a community centre in Barrhaven. The auditorium was packed with over a hundred people. They explained the process of sponsorship and allowed for a

---

3   Don Smith began sponsoring with his parish in Sillery, Quebec, in 1979 during the Southeast Asian refugee crisis. After retiring from the public service in 2003, he joined the Refugee Assistance Group at St. John the Evangelist Anglican Church in Ottawa. In 2012, he became the Chair of the Anglican Diocese of Ottawa's Refugee Working Group. Don and the Anglican Diocese's Refugee Working Group and SAH are very highly regarded across Canada for their work welcoming refuge-seekers over the years.

question and answer period at the end. Robyne recalls that despite the pace at which everything was happening across the country, these meetings were useful because of the expertise and stories faith-based and community groups could share: "It was kind of made up as we went along but there was a sponsorship infrastructure already established and that had to do with the ecumenical movement that had been going on for quite some time."

The next day, the ROC also hosted the very first session of a more advanced information meeting called "Sponsorship 201" at St. Joe's. This too was organized by Refugee 613 and the RSTP. The three-hour meeting was intended for groups that were already formed. It included cultural sensitivity training and helped sponsor groups to approach their role ethically, to navigate group dynamics, and to connect with community resources. Experienced members of the ROC were on hand to share their advice on sponsorship.

As sponsorship groups formed and submitted applications, both overseas humanitarian agencies and the federal government struggled to screen GARs and PSRs quickly enough to meet the demand. In response, the immigration department deployed about five hundred officials to the Middle East to expedite screenings and periodically posted short lists of screened refugees available for Blended Visa Office-Referred (BVOR)[4] and PSR sponsorship (Chase et al. 2015). Louise remembers that these names were snatched up within minutes by competing sponsorship groups.

Enthusiasm continued to grow in the new year. On January 11, 2016, the Parish hosted a general information meeting, and Robyne and Louise presented on the ROC's behalf to explain how parishioners could get involved in hosting and sponsorship. Forty-one people were in attendance and thirty-five interested persons sent their regrets. The ROC recognized that there were too many people interested to effectively integrate them into the ROC's main activities. Instead, they created a subcommittee dedicated to the work of

---

4   The BVOR attempts to combine the benefits of both the Government-Assisted Refugee (GAR) and Privately Sponsored Refugee (PSR) models by allowing the federal government to select refugees screened by the United Nations High Commissioner for Refugees (UNHCR), also known as the UN Refugee Agency, in countries of asylum and then matching them with private sponsors in Canada who provide for their day-to-day settlement needs during their first year in Canada. The financial cost of the sponsorship is split between sponsors and the federal government, each of whom pays for roughly half the cost of resettlement (Labman 2019; Labman and Hyndman 2019).

welcoming Syrians to Ottawa named the Parish Support for Syrian Refugees Group and chaired by Michael McBane. The subcommittee was composed of five regular members. On the advice of the ROC's experienced members, the subcommittee agreed that they would leave sponsorship to other groups and focus on immediate, practical ways of assisting Syrian refugees who had already or would shortly settle in their community. ROC leadership connected them with CCI's host program, where the new subcommittee members were each matched with GARs who could benefit from their friendship and support. All subcommittee members got police checks and CCI training before being matched. Michael recalls that at one of these training sessions he met a number of young Vietnamese Canadians whose families had come to Canada as refugees in the late 1970s. They too were eager to show solidarity with newly arrived Syrians.

The Syrian family Michael was matched with had four children ranging in age from six to twenty. The parents spoke almost no English and at first the subcommittee members communicated with them through their two eldest sons. In the early days, Michael and others helped the family get the things they needed for their home and for school. They also helped them as they navigated a succession of apartments all too small for their six-person family. Despite initial linguistic barriers, the family's English, especially the children's, improved quickly.

The subcommittee did not stop there. As members were getting matched as hosts, they began assessing what other needs existed for refugees throughout the city. Robyne became an important liaison in this regard, both for the ROC and other organizations in the city, as she worked full-time as a coordinator for the Family Reception Centre for the Ottawa-Carleton District School Board. She helped the ROC's subcommittee contact schools to understand the needs of incoming Syrian students. By March 2016, Ottawa had welcomed nearly 1,100 Syrian refugees, of which sixty percent were fourteen and under (Laucius 2016). More than three hundred of these children were enrolled in Ottawa schools. To meet their needs, the subcommittee gathered donations of backpacks, supplies, and money from parishioners. Michael recalls that parishioners responded incredibly well to this call: "A lot of people have children and they know what getting ready for school is about. They felt good that they were given a tangible, helpful suggestion on how to help the Syrian refugees as opposed to just a vague universal call for help."

The subcommittee existed for about a year and eventually dissolved back into the ROC. Subcommittee members who had been trained as hosts continued to fill their commitment to provide support to the Syrian GAR families they became friends with during this period. Over the years since, these connections have proven valuable. Michael reports that when the eldest son of the family he hosted applied for his first job, he asked Michael to serve as his reference. Michael gave the young man a glowing review and he received his first job offer in Canada. This event taught Michael a valuable lesson about being a newcomer: "Those intangible things are very important for new arrivals. Just having someone locally who can be a reference for you."

* * *

Behind the scenes of this increased Parish involvement, the revitalized ROC was working hard to meet the many requests they were receiving. They experienced a surge in donations from parishioners, community members, and partners such as the Religious of the Sacred Heart of Jesus (RSCJ; see Chapter 1). With these funds, the ROC proceeded to evaluate the many sponsorship requests they received to determine which of them to commit to.

One of these came after their Sponsorship 101 session in Barrhaven in December, when Louise and Robyne were approached by a young man of Syrian origin named Abraham. As people trickled out after the session, Abraham told the ROC duo the story of how Syria's war had affected his family. Abraham himself had immigrated to Canada around 2005 while his family remained in Syria. As war broke out in Syria, he heard the news from his family with mounting concern, speaking frequently with his sister, a single mother of two, and his parents. Despite his worries, he says he never expected what happened next.

In June 2014, his sister was out walking one day and got caught in the middle of a skirmish between the rebels and the Syrian government regime. She had spoken with Abraham on the phone that morning, and only a few hours later she was killed by an explosion. Abraham recounts the pain he and his family felt and still feel: "It was a really big shock for everyone [in] my family. She was thirty-four.... We know it's a war and we're trying our best to keep them safe. When that happened, it was ... I [can't] find the exact word to express my feelings in that moment."

Abraham recalls his grief turning to depression. To cope, he focused all his efforts on bringing his sister's two orphaned girls—then aged thirteen and fifteen—to Canada. Though the girls were being taken care of by their grandfather and, when he passed away, by their aunt, Abraham considered himself their de facto guardian.

As a student at Carleton University at the time, Abraham used his limited funds to hire a lawyer and explore every pathway to bring them to Canada. His lawyer explained that bringing them to Canada would likely prove to be "an uphill battle" and said that the government rarely allowed people to sponsor anyone outside their nuclear family, including nieces or nephews, and would, therefore, be unlikely to accept a permanent residence application based on family ties. His lawyer warned him that the federal government's position would likely be that his nieces could more easily continue to live with other family members in Syria than be uprooted to Canada.

Determined to try, in January 2015, Abraham nevertheless submitted a permanent residence application for his nieces under the family class. In the meantime, expecting to be refused, Abraham prepared a "Plan B." When the news about Alan Kurdi spread across Canada in September 2015, he began attending as many information sessions as he could about private sponsorship, imagining that if the application for permanent residency were refused, he would try to bring them as part of the twenty-five thousand refugees. This plan still had its complications, including his nieces' minor status, the high cost of sponsorship, and their residency in Syria. Abraham recalls, "I kept in touch with any church, any private sponsor, any people that were willing to help." He also offered his help as interpreter, guide, or friend, to help any other incoming Syrian refugees.

Unfortunately, but not unexpectedly, in the early fall of 2015, his nieces' application for permanent residence was refused on the grounds that they did not qualify as family members under the definition provided in the *Immigration and Refugee Protection Regulations*—and for lack of providing proof of sufficient funding. However, the immigration department offered to refer the application on humanitarian and compassionate (H&C) grounds to the Canadian embassy in Amman, Jordan, for further evaluation if Abraham wished. With this chance, Abraham was determined to do everything he could to turn the case in his favour. To save money and prove that he could take on the responsibilities of a guardian, he left university and started working three jobs.

This was the state of Abraham's affairs on the night Louise and Robyne met him at their Sponsorship 101 session. Within a week, the duo convened the ROC to discuss the possibility of helping Abraham. The members unanimously agreed that Abraham's case fit both within their mission and their budget, and they began planning to privately sponsor his nieces in the event that the H&C application was unsuccessful.

However, before the ROC had the chance to really assist in any way, in January 2016, much earlier than expected, the embassy in Amman approved Abraham's H&C application for his nieces. Abraham's persistence had won the day! He and the ROC rejoiced together. Plans to relocate his nieces moved quickly. Much had to be done. His nieces had to decide which of their possessions—symbolic of their last physical connection to their deceased mother and to their homeland—to bring with them to Canada. Abraham recognized how hard this would be for them and told them, "Whatever you want to [bring], even if it's overweight ... I'm going to pay whatever I need. Whatever is going to make you happy." In the end they brought everything, which amounted to eleven suitcases.

Next, Abraham had to organize special transportation to bring his nieces safely from Damascus, Syria, across the border to Beirut, Lebanon (a two-hour drive under good conditions). He booked himself a flight to meet them in Beirut. He recounts, "That moment I had zero dollars in my account." Looking for ways to assist, he remembers the ROC told him, "We didn't do that much about this case, but we're so happy for you ... we want to help." They offered him five thousand dollars to offset the cost of their airfare, though Abraham insisted it would only be a loan. In the weeks before his trip, they also helped him find a larger apartment and helped with other preparations.

Abraham's nieces arrived in Ottawa in February 2016, in circumstances slightly different from private sponsorships. They came not as refugees, but as Abraham's family members, making him solely responsible for their financial support. Even so, a village of supporters awaited them at the Ottawa airport: their ROC friends, Abraham's Syrian Canadian cousins and their kids, and Abraham's local Member of Parliament, to whom he had turned multiple times with requests concerning his nieces' immigration application.

Independent and proactive as always, Abraham settled well into his new life as a guardian. He recalls, however, that he was nervous about raising two teenaged girls. In this respect, the ROC could provide ample support. Robyne helped them get registered for school and liaised with their school board. Terry Byrne, a long-time parishioner and historian of St. Joe's became like an uncle to his nieces. He provided an opportunity for them to ride horses, gave them Christmas presents, and found bicycles for them. When the eldest niece was graduating from high school, the members asked Abraham what he was going to do for her prom. He remembers answering, "Why are you asking me these tough questions? I have no idea!" ROC members helped her find a dress, found someone to do her makeup, and took pictures.

The girls are now both Canadian citizens, something that makes Abraham extremely proud. He remembers when his youngest niece went to her citizenship ceremony, he cried from happiness: "I was so happy. I called all the family on WhatsApp." His niece shrugged it off, telling him that she was already Canadian even without a ceremony. "Why are you making a big deal?" she asked. Abraham responded, "Because you don't know what I did, how much I suffered to get to this moment."

Both nieces have settled well, their uncle reports, and now volunteer across the city with a number of organizations, including Refugee 613. The eldest is studying to get her bachelor's degree. Since that time, another family member has joined Abraham and his nieces in Canada. Abraham's mother, his nieces' grandmother, was permitted to enter Canada in 2017 and has since gained refugee status.

* * *

Going back to the fall of 2015, as Abraham's story with the ROC was just beginning, the ROC was approached by two couples in the Parish (who were later joined by a third from outside the Parish). They told Louise that they were interested in co-sponsoring a Syrian family with the ROC; each couple made a donation of five thousand dollars for the sponsorship and placed the funds in trust with the Committee.

Working with the ROC, the couples received a referral from CRR to privately sponsor a gay Syrian man and his three children. Since the couples had young children as well, the couples were excited about this match. However, as the Syrian family's application was being processed in Canada, the father was offered resettlement for his family by the Swiss government. Having chatted via Skype with the father and children several times, the sponsors were disappointed to some extent but happy for his success. The ROC and the couples encouraged him to accept the Swiss offer for his own safety and the future of his children.

The couples were still determined to sponsor. However, without any other personal connections to Syrian refugees, the ROC recommended that the best course of action would be to turn to the BVOR program. Implemented in 2012 under the previous federal government, the BVOR program was introduced at a time when the government was seeking to encourage private sponsorship over government-assisted sponsorship. Harper's federal government had recognized that there were two significant barriers to participation in private sponsorship: first, many Canadians did not personally know any refugees and, second, the financial cost of sponsorship was often prohibitive. To help would-be sponsors to overcome these barriers, the government constructed the BVOR program as a hybrid resettlement stream which attempted to combine the benefits of the GAR and PSR models.

Under the BVOR program, refugee referrals are made by the UNHCR, as they are for GARs, meaning that sponsors are matched with a refugee unknown to them. However, unlike GARs, who are resettled by the government and not assigned sponsors, BVORs are given sponsors who sign an agreement, much like PSR sponsors, to provide for most of the day-to-day settlement needs. The financial cost of the sponsorship is then split between sponsors and the Canadian government, each of which pays roughly half the cost of resettlement (Labman 2019; Labman and Hyndman 2019).

Although the BVOR program has been criticized by some who see it as a means for the government to shift responsibility onto private sponsors, it was immensely effective in connecting new sponsor groups with refugees abroad seeking resettlement during the Syrian Initiative. Since many Canadians were keen to sponsor but few personally knew any Syrian refugees, the BVOR program helped them to bridge this gap. It also had a number of significant benefits, including that BVOR sponsorships were generally processed more quickly, and cost-sharing with the government significantly reduced the amount of money groups had to raise. The program was tremendously popular because of these benefits, which were especially well suited to the cohort of sponsors motivated by the Syrian Initiative. Sponsors recall waiting for the BVOR list to be issued, attempting to respond fast enough to "get" a family to sponsor, and the disappointment of failing and having to wait another week (Goodyear 2015). It was in this context, Minister of Immigration John McCallum proudly proclaimed he was the only minister of immigration in the world who could not provide enough refugees to satisfy his citizens (Hicks 2016).

When the ROC and the couples' sponsorship fell through in January 2016, they turned to the BVOR list and were matched with a family of five with the last name Alkhatib living in the Azraq camp in Amman, Jordan. The ROC was told to expect the family within two or three months as part of the 25,000 promised by Trudeau's Liberal government. Soon after being matched, Robyne spoke to Amir, the father, over the phone, explaining the sponsorship process: "[When we called] he did not know that we were sponsoring him and that we were anxiously awaiting his arrival. He was relieved to hear that his name was known" (ROC Archives 2016). Yet, due to rigorous security checks, the family's approval was continuously delayed. The ROC even lost a deposit they had put down on an apartment. Amir remembers, "I started buying things and preparing myself but then I had to wait for [nearly] a year and a half."

The Alkhatib family finally arrived in March 2017. One of the sponsoring couples offered to have them live in their home for the first few weeks as Amir and ROC members searched together for a suitable apartment. Maha, the mother, remembers, "At the beginning there was a lot of fear. I was pretty sad too and I was really stressed, but later I started to get used to it. We stayed with them for the first period of time ... and they were very nice to us. I started to calm down." She remembers her worries about how people would perceive her commitment to the hijab: "I was worried about how people would look at me, but everybody was respecting me."

A settlement plan was devised, and the ROC divided volunteers into a number of teams to concentrate on different facets of the family's settlement, including orientation, housing, finances, clothing, furniture, groceries, transportation, interpretation, cultural and social activities, employment, and health. ROC members helped the family get their children enrolled and thriving in school. Margie Cain, an ROC member who joined in the spring of 2015, remembers scouring Kijiji looking for suitable apartments: "[We] realized how many dollars it takes to have a decent type of apartment in 2016–2017 that you would want to welcome a family into in terms of comfort, security, neighbourhood, and everything else." Dorothy Collins helped Maha study English and taught her to sew, just as she had taught Sarah to sew while she was in sanctuary twelve years earlier. A Muslim friend from the local community helped them find a mosque to attend and showed them where to buy halal food. Others equipped them with winter gear, so they could survive Ottawa in mid-March. Amir recalls, "[The ROC] actually removed a lot of the challenges that we would have faced without them."

This broad range of settlement support is not uncommon for active, enthusiastic sponsors of PSRs and BVORs. Amir noted that the support they received was not what all Syrians have experienced, especially for the GARs he knows: "They get people sometimes from maybe the government that check on them maybe once a month and there wasn't that much support. While on the other hand, us, the group was with us all the time." Some preliminary evidence suggests that as a result of this hands-on support, PSRs integrate more quickly into Canadian life and, over their lifetime, do better according to standard measures of integration. Yet PSRs and BVORs, like the Alkhatib family, still may not feel at home in their new community (Hyndman, Payne, and Jimenez 2016; Kaida, Hou, and Stick 2020). Amir remembers that a few months after his arrival, a ROC member asked him why he did not go out more frequently to meet other people.

Amir explained that he did not go out because he knew no one and missed his family. He openly wondered if the ROC could help him bring more of his family to Canada, specifically his cousin who he said was like a brother to him. This cousin was also married to Maha's sister—therefore, both Amir and Maha had deep family ties at stake in this proposition. The ROC member who had this conversation with Amir passed this information on to the other committee members. They discussed it briefly but agreed that since their BVOR commitment to the Alkhatib family was ongoing (for a period of twelve months after their arrival), they could not consider another sponsorship at least until the twelve months had elapsed.

When the year was over, Amir asked again. This time the ROC could agree. They submitted an application to privately sponsor Amir's cousin and his family of six in spring 2018. The application was approved fairly quickly—their arrival being set for October 2018.

After this good news, the ROC and Amir began looking for housing. Both the ROC and the Alkhatib family had first-hand experience with the competitive housing market in Ottawa. Since their arrival, the Alkhatibs had been living in a townhouse that was too small for the five of them, with a baby on the way. They had been unable to find anything else that matched their needs and their budget.

With this in mind, John Weir set up a meeting with the Alkhatibs' property manager to see if a three-bedroom apartment could be found in their neighbourhood. The manager had good news. One of their properties had just become available and was being renovated with new paint and floors. Even better, the house was available for October 1, 2018, and the family was set to arrive October 3. The timing could scarcely have been more perfect. The only drawback was that the property was not in the Alkhatibs' neighbourhood.

John remembers a bittersweet experience he had with Amir when they went to view the townhouse for his cousin:

> It was actually so sad because [Amir] and I went and it was like going into a brand new house … a very nice area … and there was a swimming pool right across the street from them. And we go in and it smelled like a brand new house. The fresh paint, the floors were all ripped out but they were putting a new flooring and all that stuff … we walk up and we see the master bedroom.

They walked around the house and Amir was clearly pleased that this would be a wonderful home for his cousin's family. He remarked that his young daughter would have loved having a room of her own, saying "I wish we had this…. Wow, they're coming to a house that is better than mine."

Thankfully, since their cousins' arrival, the Alkhatibs have moved into a three-bedroom townhouse in the same neighbourhood. His daughter now has her own room and doesn't have to share with her brothers anymore.

The joy of being reunited has made all the difference, Amir and Maha report. Maha recounts that being apart from her family weighed heavily on her, especially when she was pregnant during her first year in Canada. She worried because she had never gone through pregnancy without family support. She wanted her children to grow up with grandparents. Though the ROC helped her get to doctors' appointments (even on the day of her delivery) and Dorothy Collins became her children's Canadian grandmother, it was still hard to be without their family. The ROC's Margie put it this way, "They made the best of it but there is that sense of leaving something behind. So many brothers, so many sisters, so many cousins. So much of your culture and your life." When the Alkhatibs' cousins finally arrived, Maha recalls: "It was a wonderful thing.... I really can't tell you exactly. It was a really, really wonderful thing."

These and many other opportunities came to the ROC as public interest in helping Syrian refugees swelled. Along with these sponsorships, the ROC met with many people seeking assistance in sponsoring friends or families abroad whom community members and organizations referred to them. In September 2016, the CCI contacted the ROC to seek support for a GAR family of eight: two parents with six children, ranging from one to seventeen years of age. The family had arrived as part of the 25,000 in January 2016. Two of the younger children had specific medical needs and were being monitored by the Children's Hospital of Eastern Ontario (CHEO). They needed assistance travelling to and from their many medical appointments, as well as with learning English, orienting themselves to the city, and budgeting. Committee member Frank O'Brien, together with his wife Doris, began to meet the parents weekly for ninety-minute English lessons. To this day, Frank and Doris still maintain a strong friendship with this family.

* * *

The years of the Syrian Initiative, which formally lasted until about 2017 when the twelve-month period for the majority of private sponsorships elapsed, revitalized the settlement sector and community groups throughout Canada. Despite valid criticism for aspects of its delivery, the initiative was considered an extraordinary feat (Labman and Cameron 2020; Hamilton, Veronis, and Walton-Roberts 2020). An estimated forty thousand private sponsors in communities and organizations participated across Canada (Macklin et al. 2018). A diverse range of volunteers and organizations with a range of motivations and experiences were part of this extraordinary effort to extend safety and welcome to strangers.

In Toronto, Mohammad Al Zaibak, a Syrian Canadian telecommunications leader, founded a non-profit organization called Lifeline Syria. This organization helped facilitate and successfully complete the processing of sponsorship applications for 1,200 Syrians. In Guelph, Joe Estill, a local entrepreneur, has sponsored over 130 families—eighty-nine of whom are Syrian—since 2015 (Keung 2019). In Pictou County, Nova Scotia, a new group called Safe Harbour resettled nine refugee families (seven Syrian and two Congolese). In Whitehorse, Yukon, a group formed in September 2015 has since welcomed four Syrian families in their community (Croft 2018).

In Ottawa, the community collaborated to resettle over two thousand Syrian refugees between November 2015 and the end of 2016 (OLIP 2017). Today, citizens and residents across the city continue to take on second, third, fourth, or more sponsorships. In one incredible effort, a faith-based sponsorship group in Ottawa worked together to facilitate eight sponsorships to reunite over thirty-five family members in eastern Ontario (Morris, Lenard, and Haugen 2021).

The Syrian Initiative also revitalized the ROC. Many new Committee members joined during this time while a number of others moved on to other things. The experience gained during the Syrian Initiative helped to create successors and leaders to continue the groundwork laid by the ROC's first generation of leaders, including Louise, Pierre, Irene, and many others. Parallel to these events, Robyne and Louise, true to their word, anchored the leadership of the ROC, with John joining them along the way, till the time of a general meeting, which came about in June 2017. At the meeting, John was elected chair and chose Margie Cain and Angela Murphy to form the leadership team with him. John, with Robyne, provided experience and continuity when Louise retired at the end of the year. She remains a Committee member at heart, always available to offer guidance or to fill in the blanks on the ROC's history as the need arises.

The number of refugees worldwide has only grown in recent years, making the work of volunteers in the settlement sector all the more vital. With this in mind, the next chapter examines the current state of volunteerism and refugee settlement both for the ROC and across Canada.

CHAPTER 5

Longevity

What would be different today if the Refugee Outreach Committee's (ROC's) founding members had never attended the archdiocesan symposium on immigrants and refugees in 1990? What if St. Joe's Parish had not supported and sustained the ROC's initiative? The ROC's stories are a testament to two phenomena within Canada's settlement sector. The first is that the everyday choices of a small number of dedicated, ordinary people (immigrants, private individuals, community groups, etc.) can bring about extraordinary waves of change in the lives of others and in Canada's policies and politics. The second, related, phenomenon is that because of the groundwork laid by ordinary people like these, Canada has had major success in harnessing en masse socio-political movements led by refugee advocates, such as those in 1978 and 2015, to protect people seeking refuge from around the world.

Since 1990, the ROC has hosted over sixty-five families, totalling more than one hundred and sixty people. They have also privately sponsored seven families and four individuals, totalling over thirty people, through the PSRP and the Joint Assistance Sponsorship (JAS) program—thirty people who may not have been able to find refuge in Canada (or elsewhere) if the ROC had not advocated for them. Additionally, through their affiliation with the CCI—the ROC's Sponsorship Agreement Holder (SAH)—the ROC has acted as a co-sponsor and guarantor for more than fifteen other private sponsorships since 2001 by holding funds in trust for other community sponsor groups and assisting them with the application process.

The ROC also played an important role in advocating for refugee claimants in Ottawa and at a national level. They provided sanctuary, spoke at parliamentary committee meetings, and provided support to refugee claimants who had very little other support. The ROC has directly assisted twenty-five refugee claimants since 1990 and has made a concerted effort to reach out to many more on an ad hoc basis, especially in recent years, as claims have increased. Through these actions, ROC members learned about the deep injustices embedded in the Canadian refugee determination system. Although a Refugee Appeal Division (RAD) exists today, refugee claimants still face many individual and systemic barriers while seeking asylum in Canada. These barriers include the biases of single-member adjudication panels; lack of access to legal representation in both the initial decision process and in appeals, removals, etc.; and policies that prevent asylum seekers from even reaching Canada in the first place, like the Canada–U.S. Safe Third Country Agreement or direct-back policies during the COVID-19 pandemic (CCR 2012; LaViolette 2014; CCR 2021; Paperny 2021).

The existence of such barriers—and the expanding number of displaced and refuge-seeking people worldwide—indicates that there is a continued and growing need for refugee advocates in Canada today.

In Ottawa, the ROC is still very active. Current co-chair, Margie Cain, reports that the ROC is still committed to several sponsorships, a number of which are for Syrian refuge-seekers, and continues to field the many other regular requests they receive to assist refugee claimants and GARs. Yet when we last interviewed her, Margie felt that the ROC was ready for a little bit of "down time" after a few years of intense involvement. Despite the ROC's successes and experiences, their stories also demonstrate how volunteer groups naturally change over time and experience periods of high and low activity.

As we have seen with the ROC, many of the services and programs in the settlement sector are run by volunteers who give their time, for no pay and often outside of regular work hours, to support the integration of refugees (Wilson 2012; Verba, Schlozman, and Brady 1995; Gouthro 2010). Volunteer and community participation in the settlement sector have long been and still are vital to advocacy for and with refuge-seekers. Louisa Taylor, Director of the Ottawa-based organization Refugee 613, says that protecting the efforts of groups like the ROC is essential:

> The team at St. Joe's has just created this rich, priceless commu-
> nity asset. I remember being at an event that Louise Lalonde
> spoke at. Here are these ... presumably middle-class, average
> citizens who have done extraordinary work for people they
> didn't know. Those folks are amazing and there are lots of them
> across Canada. But in any one community they are not so com-
> mon and so you have to find ways to protect their efforts so that
> they don't feel like they are shouting into the wind and having
> trouble bringing people into this incredible experience.

Retaining volunteers—and private sponsors—is especially important right now. Participation in settlement and private sponsorship is still significantly high and the Canadian public is increasingly supportive of immigration and refuge-seekers (Environics 2020). This window of opportunity places government and refugee advocates in an ideal position to design a more robust and supportive environment for vol-unteers for years to come.

Still, public attention to refugee resettlement is not as high as it was in 2015. Waning interest is not unusual, but it is also not inevita-ble. A report released in June 2021 by the Environics Institute for Survey Research in partnership with Refugee 613 indicates that public awareness and interest in private sponsorship is still very high. Nearly one-fifth of people surveyed indicated that they would definitely (2%) or likely (15%) see themselves participating in private sponsorship in the near future (Environics 2021). If this survey is representative, it means that a pool of approximately four million Canadian residents are willing to participate in sponsorship in the near future, a happy fact given the imminent arrival of thousands of Afghan refugees to Canada (Keung 2021). With this in mind, determining the factors that condition participation in private sponsorship is extremely important for bringing new volunteers into the program.

Any decline in participation should also not be mistaken for an actual decline in the number of people seeking refuge and protection across the world. Refugee populations are only increasing. In 2019, according to official statistics published by the United Nations High Commissioner for Refugees (UNHCR) and the United Nations Relief and Works Agency (UNRWA), there were at least 4,723,111 more people seeking refuge than in 2015 (UNHCR, n.d.). There are an estimated 5.5 million Syrian refuge-seekers now, compared to 4 million in 2015. Beyond Syria, an incomprehensible number of refuge-seekers have left their countries while receiving much less media and political attention, including from Venezuela, Somalia, South Sudan, and Myanmar. In addition, many hundreds of thousands of refuge-seekers across East Africa have been living in camps for decades in protracted refugee situations (Milner and Loescher 2011).

Though the surge of public and government support for refugees gained during the Syrian Initiative was certainly commendable, the need today for resettlement and other durable solutions for refuge-seekers is just as strong. Providing protection to refuge-seekers is likely to be a permanent aspect of governance—in Canada and every nation—for many years to come. If the federal government plans to continue to rely on private sponsors, they must provide robust support to sustain both historic volunteers and new volunteers gained during and after 2015. Louisa, of Refugee 613, says there is a need to understand what motivates and incentivizes people to sponsor:

> It's not easy. It takes a certain kind of person to sponsor. I think a lot of the people who came to it in 2015–2016, who came to it with all the good will, are exhausted. Sponsorship burnout is real. People are always asking us about marketing and mobilization of sponsors, but we tell them that the product has to be really good. If it leaves sponsors burned out and jaded, then you aren't going to have people acting as ambassadors for your program.

If the government wants to prevent burnout and bad experiences, it is essential to understand *who* is willing to sponsor and volunteer and to understand *why* they do it and *what* motivates them to continue doing it.

Understanding the factors that condition participation and success is also important now as the Canadian government, the UNHCR, and partners are seeking to promote the spread of sponsorship to other countries as a "complementary pathway" for refugee protection. The Global Refugee Sponsorship Initiative (GRSI) was launched in 2016 with the goal of exporting Canada's private sponsorship model and thereby encouraging international responsibility-sharing, expanding refugee resettlement, and mobilizing citizens in direct support of refuge-seekers (UNHCR 2016). But can private sponsorship be successful elsewhere, and which of the program's characteristics are essential? There are a number of Canadian characteristics which may not be easily replicated in the short term, including Canada's fairly pro-immigration citizens and political parties, its ability to control irregular migration due to its relative isolation, and high public demand for resettlement (Smith 2020). However, St. Joe's experiences may provide some context to explain what motivates and sustains private sponsors.

After all these years, how does the ROC account for its longevity? Clearly an important element is its members' dedication and adaptability, evident in the way they responded quickly to requests for assistance and adjusted to volunteer turnover, new policies, and cancelled or urgent sponsorships. During the ongoing COVID-19 pandemic, Committee members have demonstrated unprecedented adaptability as they continue to build friendships and support refuge-seekers and newcomers through virtual English lessons, physically distanced social outings, bike rides, picnics in the park, and supply drop-offs.

The ROC's longevity might also be attributed, in part, to St. Joe's institutional structure and support. The ROC's affiliation with a faith-based organization like St. Joe's has given them a place to meet each month for the past thirty years. It has given them access to Parish bank accounts, a photocopying machine, a membership to recruit from, and more. Additionally, St. Joe's commitment to public ministry, which includes the ROC, the Supper Table and the Women's Centre, provided the ROC an institutional safety net to encourage its continued work while affording the ROC ample freedom to operate under its own direction. In challenging times, the ROC could rely on the Parish's interventions, as they did in 2013, when the ROC nearly dissolved, and Mary Murphy was appointed by the Parish Council to revitalize it.

However, ROC members reported that volunteer motivation is affected by a slew of challenges that range from mundane and bureaucratic to cultural and interpersonal. This is common among private sponsors. Many face the difficulties of finding affordable and appropriate housing for the individuals and families they assist, as well as long and uncertain waiting periods throughout the sponsorship process, insufficient information about refugees prior to arrival, extensive paperwork and accounting, and navigating discomfort or disagreements related to cultural differences (Clarke and Marlow 2020; Kyriakides et al. 2018). Despite the great love many sponsors have for their role, many feel isolated from government and government-funded support and services (Blain et al. 2019). They feel like they have to find answers to settlement challenges alone—not always because there is no support but because they are unaware of services they could have accessed to help Privately Sponsored Refugees (PSRs).

Refuge-seekers and their sponsors can be particularly frustrated by the difficulties of finding employment or transferring credentials from one country to the next. Rabbi Elizabeth Bolton, who helps lead a sponsorship group called Rainbow Haven in Ottawa, suggests that employment is one of the major pressure points for groups as they approach month thirteen—the month when sponsors stop providing financial assistance. Additionally, inadequate access or care through government services (i.e., for health, dental, housing, educational, and employment support) often places the weight (and cost) of these deficiencies on refuge-seekers—and by extension, on the volunteers and sponsors helping them.

The barriers which prevent refuge-seekers from accessing services, supports, and opportunities after arrival are inseparably connected with the retention of volunteers and other actors in this work. Don Smith, who coordinated the Anglican Diocese's Refugee Working Group from 2012 to 2020 (a committee with broad experience that precedes the founding of the ROC), feels that the increasingly complex procedures and protocols required by the government may curtail volunteer enthusiasm. Don got involved in settlement work after retiring from his professional career and then spent the next eight years advocating for refuge-seekers. At the height of the Syrian Initiative, he spent approximately sixty hours a week dedicated to unpaid settlement work. During his time with the Diocese, the Refugee Working Group helped sponsor over nine hundred refugees. In the years since, he has noticed a drastic increase in paperwork for community groups like the Refugee Working Group and feels that an overly heavy burden of accounting and paperwork has been placed on volunteers. As further evidence, since his retirement, the Diocese has hired an additional caseworker to continue managing the Anglican Diocese's settlement work, bringing the total staff in the Refugee Ministry Office to two full-time paid employees plus volunteers.

This extra work stems from recent changes in policy around the administration of the PSRP, which for many years went relatively "unmonitored." Don reports that the public and the government have

had misgivings in recent years about whether some PSRs were receiving adequate support from their sponsors or whether they were not
getting the promised money upon arrival. In 2015, under an enor-
mous amount of pressure to ensure accountability during the Syrian
Initiative, the federal immigration department began requiring
private sponsors to provide a sponsorship settlement plan with information regarding budgeting, in particular, as well as with respect to
how various integration tasks would be accomplished. Presently,
since COVID-19 crosses borders freely even though refuge-seekers do
not, private sponsors must also provide a robust quarantine plan
before those they are sponsoring board their flights to Canada.
Although all these measures may be necessary, the government must
also evaluate how they affect sponsor motivation.

Assessing the factors that impact motivation is increasingly
important as the government continues to increase its reliance on private sponsors year by year. The Liberal government's multi-year
immigration plan for 2021–2023 suggests that it intends to continue to
resettle far more refugees through private sponsorship than through
government assistance in the coming years (IRCC 2020b). PSR targets
for 2021 are set for 22,500, whereas Government-Assisted Refugee
(GAR) targets are set for 12,500. This number is down significantly
from the more than 23,500 GARs resettled in 2016.

Refugee advocates warn that having lower GAR quotas (versus
higher PSR quotas) represents a shift toward "privatizing" Canada's
resettlement work (Ritchie 2018; Blain et al. 2019). This fundamentally
challenges the unwritten principle at the foundation of collaborations
between civil society and the federal government through the Private
Sponsorship of Refugees Program (PSRP) since the creation of the lat-
ter: that of "additionality" (Hyndman, Payne, and Jimenez 2016;
Cameron 2021, 159; CCR 2014). Additionality requires that the number
of refugees who arrive in Canada with the financial support and care
of private sponsorship groups should be "additional" to—or over and
above—the GAR quota set by the Canadian government. In other
words, the efforts of private individuals to fund and assist resettlement should not relieve the federal government of its commitment to
do the same. Canadian refugee advocates have zealously defended
this principle over many years. Refugee advocacy groups (such as the
Canadian Council for Refugees and Citizens for Public Justice) argue
that, at a time when the global need for resettlement is higher than
ever, the government's commitment to providing protection should

not decrease—even if faith-based and community organizations like the ROC are eager to increase their contribution through private sponsorship. They have called on the federal government to raise the GAR target to at least 20,000 to place it on par with that for PSRs (CCR 2017; Kaduuli 2020).

The trend toward privatizing sponsorship will likely continue, especially if the Conservative Party of Canada (CPC) is reelected. In the 2021 snap election, CPC leader Erin O'Toole's platform stated that his government's goal would be to eliminate government sponsorship as we know it today and focus almost entirely on private sponsorship and "joint sponsorship", stating: "All refugees in Canada will do so under private or joint sponsorship programs, with exceptions in cases of emergency or specific programs" (CPC 2021). However, these plans have been criticized by refugee advocates who argue that eliminating GAR sponsorship would lead to the exclusion of a whole range of vulnerable refuge-seekers who can usually be more easily sponsored under the GAR program (i.e., large families, families with high medical needs, etc.) (The Canadian 2021). Additionally, this shift would likely require recruiting a much larger cohort of private sponsors across Canada. On this note, the CPC pledged that funding would be redirected to support sponsors, with more support for SAHs with a "demonstrable track record" in settlement – likely referring to Christian SAHs, like the Mennonite Central Committee, that have historically led in sponsorship. In our view, doing so would be ill-advised without first putting a great deal of thought into *how* the government will recruit the necessary number of sponsors to maintain Canada's current level of resettlement, considering Canada's shifting demographics in religion and age.

Sponsor motivation may also be affected, both positively and negatively, by the second unwritten principle of the PSRP: selection. The PSRP has long allowed sponsors to "name" or select an individual for sponsorship—just as the ROC did when they chose to sponsor Amir Alkhatib's cousin. Being able to select a person to sponsor seems to be an important motivator for Canadian sponsors. Sponsors are generally more likely to sponsor if they can help resettle refugees that have family ties with people who are already in their community (Denton 2016). Outside times of crisis, the private sponsorship program is primarily used for family reunification; at least ninety-five percent of sponsorships before 2003 were for extended family members or friends (Labman 2016).

The strength of selection-based motivation is also demonstrated by the way the Blended Visa Office-Referred (BVOR) program's popularity has decreased significantly since 2017. BVOR is essentially a type of private sponsorship without selection: the federal government matches sponsorship groups with refugees abroad. In 2018, the government set a BVOR quota of 1,500; by August of 2018, a thousand of those spots were still unclaimed. To incentivize sponsors, the Shapiro Foundation, an American philanthropic organization, and other donors offered to cover the necessary funding for any group willing to sponsor BVOR-listed refugees in order to prevent the BVOR quota from being wasted (Lindsay 2018). This effectively reduced the cost of sponsorship to nearly zero for sponsoring groups (Refugee Hub 2019). Still, in the end, only 1,157 BVORs were resettled that year. The Shapiro Foundation made this same funding incentive available again the following year to mitigate the same problem. Clearly, the BVOR program is not incentivizing participation in sponsorship as it should. In response to the program's underperformance, the annual BVOR quota has been reduced to one thousand going forward. The loss of selection is likely at the heart of the BVORs lack of success, since it does not allow sponsors to take on family reunification cases. Selecting known family members or friends makes sense from sponsors' perspective (Morris, Lenard, and Haugen 2021). After resettling one family, sponsors often learn of other family members abroad who need the very same kind of protection. The personal relationships that sponsors develop with PSRs are strong motivators to help them reunite. In some cases, taking on family reunification sponsorships may also be less work, since refugees are greeted in Canada not only by their sponsors but their family members, who can take on some of the work of introducing them to their new city, helping them navigate settlement, and sharing language and culture.

However, private sponsors' preference for selection-based sponsorship also has its disadvantages. In a scenario where the federal government prioritizes PSR quotas over GARs, the result is a very ad hoc selection system that may not prioritize resettlement for the most vulnerable. Such a system has generally favoured family reunification, meaning that vulnerable refugees abroad who have no prior family or personal connection to Canada end up having fewer opportunities for resettlement. Additionally, the ability to select refugees opens the possibility of discriminatory selection based on religion, ethnicity, family size, and other features; whereas GARs are recommended by the

UNHCR based on their vulnerability (without preference for religion), PSRs are selected by individuals—and organizations—with possible personal preferences and connections to particular groups of displaced people. Since a large number of individuals and faith-based organizations participating in sponsorship are Christian, the system has, at times, favoured Christian refuge-seekers, though tracking such trends is difficult (Bramadat 2014; Berthiaume 2015; Levitz 2015).

In this kind of system, private sponsors are given the fraught moral responsibility of choosing which refuge-seekers should be allotted the scarce resources of resettlement (Lenard 2020, 2021). Giving private sponsors this decision shifts the government's responsibility for protecting refuge-seekers onto private citizens—who have their own opinions, priorities, and potential biases (Morris, Lenard, and Haugen 2021). For sponsor groups, the role of reuniting families can be both a great joy and a heavy responsibility. For the ROC, the decision to reunite the Alkhatib family with their cousins was not without its challenges; it required them to confront complicated ethical and moral questions. The ROC first had to determine how to balance their desire to help their new friends with responding to the many requests they continue to receive for assistance. ROC member Radamis Zaky remembers that around the same time as the ROC was discussing the sponsorship of the Alkhatibs' extended family, they received a request from a community partner who asked if the ROC would be able to privately sponsor a single woman with children in Lebanon. The members debated the merits of both cases: some felt that it would be easier to facilitate the sponsorship for the Alkhatibs' family members since they would have a network upon which to build. Some ROC members also felt that due to their close personal relationship with the Alkhatibs, it would be quite difficult to say no to them. On the other hand, the single mother's needs were pressing—and she had young children to take care of. After balancing these factors, the ROC chose to sponsor the Alkhatibs' family members.

* * *

The above challenges must be addressed in order to lighten the responsibilities currently placed on the volunteers—who are too vital to the settlement sector's capacity and structure to be lost. There are, in addition, challenges which may seem minor now but could be significant in years to come. Canada's volunteers are aging, and faith congregations are dwindling. Though there is a significant gap in representative data concerning who volunteers in the settlement sector, studies on Canada's broader volunteer sector show that there is a significant relationship between volunteerism and religiosity. Data from the most recent (2010) study on Canadian non-profit volunteerism indicates that nearly two-thirds of Canadian volunteers (over age fifteen) attended religious services at least once a week. Religious volunteers dedicated, on average, 202 hours of service in 2010, compared to the non-religious who volunteered only 141 hours, or forty percent fewer hours, on average. Additionally, Canada's most active volunteers in all sectors are among the healthy elderly (Vézina and Crompton 2012; Turcotte 2015). On average, younger adults aged twenty-five to thirty-four recorded only about one-half as many hours as seniors (109 hours versus 223 hours) (Vézina and Crompton 2012).

We can hypothesize, through limited data and anecdotal evidence, that Canadian volunteers in the settlement sector have generally followed the same patterns: they are more likely to be part of faith communities and to be among the healthy elderly. In terms of religiosity, we see this suggested in the way the majority of SAHs across Canada are linked to faith-based organizations; in 2014, an estimated seventy-two percent were faith-based (Chapman 2014). Of the six SAHs located in Ottawa, five are faith-based.[1] Though there is little data about sponsors themselves, one preliminary study conducted in 2018, based on a survey of 530 private sponsors, suggests that during the Syrian Initiative, sponsors were most likely to be highly educated, older women of European ancestry (Macklin et al. 2018). Of the respondents, seventy-four percent were women, seventy-four percent were fifty or older, and thirty-six percent identified as retired. When asked why they had joined a sponsorship group, thirty-eight percent said it was due to shared faith. This was only exceeded by forty-three percent who came together through "family, friendship, and neighbourhood networks," in keeping with what was to be expected during the surge of new community sponsorships during the Syrian Initiative.

---

1   Ottawa's six SAHs are the Catholic Centre for Immigrants (Catholic), the Ethiopian Evangelical Church in Ottawa (Evangelical), the Incorporated Synod of the Diocese of Ottawa (Anglican), the Roman Catholic Episcopal Corporation of Ottawa (Catholic), the St. Elias Antiochian Orthodox Society of Ottawa (Orthodox), and the World University Service of Canada (WUSC) - Student Refugee Program (secular).

The results of this survey may not be entirely representative of the more than forty thousand private sponsors who undertook sponsorships between 2015 and 2017 in Canada—nor is it fully representative of the cohort of sponsors that came before them, who were more likely to take on family sponsorships (Denton 2016). Still, whatever the number of faith-based volunteers, it is essential to recognize that faith communities have long held a privileged, influential place in Canada's settlement sector. This was evident in the way the federal government partnered with faith communities after World War II and during the Southeast Asian refugee movement of the late 1970s to create the PSRP (Cameron 2020; Enns, Good Gingrich, and Perez 2020; Molloy et al. 2017). It was evident across Canada, when churches and faith communities were able to provide sanctuary fifty times between 1983 and 2009 (and many more times since) without being criminally charged (Lippert 2005b; Lippert 2009). For the ROC, it was evident when they were asked, alongside a number of faith communities across Canada, to speak repeatedly at Parliamentary and Senate committees (in discussions that featured no refuge-seekers, we should note).

The centrality of faith communities in settlement is important to examine, because there has been a clear decline in religious commitment among Canadians in recent years. In the 2011 census, 23.9 percent of the Canadian population reported no religious affiliation; a decade earlier 16.5 percent said the same (Statistics Canada 2016). Declining religiosity may pose a significant challenge to a sector that has long been led by faith-based, particularly Christian, communities and organizations (Cameron 2021). The settlement sector has been built on the assumption that faith communities will be major partners in delivering services. The ROC also observed this change and wondered how declining religiosity in Canada might affect their work. As Margie Cain put it: "We [the ROC] sort of exist because of our church structure in a way. And I think St. Joe's is a vibrant community and it is likely going to outlast many, but a number of church communities have had to just shut down."

Additional changes due to Canada's aging population may also increase the settlement sector's need to adapt in years to come. Don Smith has noticed a "greying," or aging, of sponsors in recent years and feels that it is important to continue bringing in new people (though not necessarily young people) to the work. Though many new people began participating during the Syrian Initiative, this initial engagement by no means ensures their continued participation.

For leaders and refugee advocates, now is the time to find ways both to strengthen existing volunteer networks and to develop new ways of recruiting and engaging volunteers.

Going forward, it will be vital for the Canadian government to re-evaluate their assumptions about the resettlement sector, private sponsorship, and the volunteers they rely on. In 2019, Canada resettled thirty thousand refuge-seekers—more than any other resettlement country. Of these thirty thousand, a little over twenty thousand were privately sponsored (through the PSRP and the BVOR) (Government of Canada 2020b). If the government hopes to increasingly rely on private sponsors and to do so in the long term, they will need to account for declining religiosity across Canada.

One solution is to encourage the diversification of volunteers in sponsorship and settlement services. There are already emerging avenues through which the government can do so. Settlement work is increasingly being taken on by secular or identity-based community groups across Canada. Many such groups have emerged over the years and are gaining legitimacy and influence both with the government and the public. In Ottawa in 2010, Lisa Hébert and the late Nicole LaViolette founded Capital Rainbow Refuge (CRR) in an effort to increase the number of LGBTQ+ refuge-seekers resettled in Canada. LaViolette, a law professor at the University of Ottawa, had been involved for over eighteen years in training decision makers at the Immigration and Refugee Board (IRB) on how to sensitively make decisions about LGBTQ+ asylum claims. Hébert, her partner, had previously been a producer for the Canadian Broadcast Corporation (CBC). After LaViolette wrote an op-ed in the *Globe and Mail* in the summer of 2010 encouraging the queer community to get involved in sponsorship, she and Hébert gathered a diverse group of friends, professionals, lawyers, and law students to form CRR (LaViolette 2010).

CRR has been sponsoring LGBTQ+ refugees ever since and now also offers ad hoc support to refugees whose support has collapsed. Today, CRR is a non-profit organization that supports twenty sponsorship groups across the National Capital Region and Eastern Ontario. Each of these groups ranges from five to twenty-five volunteers. Together, they have sponsored more than a hundred LGBTQ+ refugees and helped hundreds more. Until recently, the organization was completely volunteer run, but some recent grants have allowed CRR to hire its first staff. In 2020, CRR also received a COVID-19 grant from the federal government, allowing them to hire four temporary staff and to distribute aid to people who have lost income due to COVID-19. Rabbi Liz Bolton from Rainbow Haven, one of the smaller sponsorship groups trained by CRR, says that having CRR's support is a model with great benefits: CRR mentors and takes on the weight of advocacy with the government and ministries so that sponsor groups can focus on the frontline work of settlement.

Many other LGBTQ+ advocates have formed similar groups across Canada. In 2011, the federal government partnered with the Rainbow Refugee Society, based in Vancouver, to establish a unique blended-refugee sponsorship program called the Rainbow Refugee Assistance Pilot. The program incentivizes participation in sponsorship by covering the costs of the first three months of settlement, while sponsors fundraise for the next nine (RSTP, n.d.). This pilot was formalized as the Rainbow Refugee Assistance Partnership (or Rainbow RAP) in 2019 when a number of LGBTQ+ organizations under the name Rainbow Coalition 4 Refuge lobbied the federal government to make the pilot permanent. The Rainbow RAP, which the federal government has committed to funding for five years starting in 2020, continues to cover three months of government funding for up to fifty applications each year, whereas previously, applications were capped at fifteen (IRCC 2019). Additionally, applications for LGBTQ+ refugees over and above fifty can still be accepted under this program, though they will not receive government funding. This cost-sharing model is another important recognition of the legitimacy that secular groups have gained over the years. The blossoming of LGBTQ+ sponsorship groups across the country demonstrates how the actions of a few people have snowballed and also suggests that government support of private sponsors, such as that available under the Rainbow RAP, can help engage volunteers in the long term.

Another group demonstrating the growing new cohort of secular actors is Operation Ezra, based in Winnipeg. In 2015, a group of Yazidi and Jewish community members formed a secular partnership to advocate for Yazidi resettlement after the massacre of thousands of Yazidi men and the abduction of thousands of women and girls by Daesh (also known as ISIS) in northern Iraq in the summer of 2014. Yazidi Canadians across Canada (but mostly based in Winnipeg and London) mounted an effective campaign to convince the federal government to fast-track the resettlement and protection of escaped Yazidi refugees, many of whom had survived terrible atrocities and sex trafficking. Against this backdrop, Operation Ezra began as a small grassroots collaboration to privately sponsor family members (Pearlman 2020). It has since grown into a coalition with over forty partners across Winnipeg, from local churches and synagogues to local businesses and even corporations like IKEA. As of February 2020, eleven family units (seventy-three individuals) have been resettled. Pearlman writes that the resources, investment, and support available because of these multi-level partnerships and a bottom-up, community engagement approach have allowed Operation Ezra to continue expanding and evolving. This organization has increasingly gained government support. In 2018, Operation Ezra secured more than one hundred thousand dollars in federal government funding in addition to private donations. Additionally, by 2017, Canada's Yazidi community convinced Canada to resettle 1,216 GARs and eighty-eight PSRs who had survived Daesh atrocities (Government of Canada 2018). As ethnic diversity increases in Canada, these kinds of temporary or permanent groups could become major sources of expertise, influence, and sustainability for the settlement sector, as Christian faith communities have been in the past.

Student groups across Canada have sought to get involved in refugee sponsorship and settlement work. One avenue for participation is campus chapters of the World University Service of Canada's (WUSC) Student Refugee Program, which combines youth-to-youth resettlement support and post-secondary education opportunities for young refugees. Though the WUSC has been active since 1978, it experienced a surge in participation across Canada in 2015. In 2016, campus chapters sponsored the resettlement of about 160 refugee students. Today, WUSC chapters across ninety campuses sponsor about 130 students per year (WUSC, n.d.), whereas in 2010 they sponsored about sixty (Plasterer 2010). Though many universities have continued to participate since the Syrian Initiative, this participation is by no means guaranteed in the long term, especially when considering the disruption caused by COVID-19. How can campus groups be better supported to ensure that they continue to participate in the long term? Christina Clark-Kazak, a professor and WUSC faculty advisor at the University of Ottawa, has been involved with WUSC since 2014. She feels that it is important for actors in the settlement sector to avoid having a "flavour of the month" approach to resettlement. This requires balancing the sponsorship of refugees from conflicts receiving high media attention (like Syrians or Rohingya) with those from protracted and less publicized situations. WUSC has generally been able to achieve this balance over the years because of historical links to communities that can make referrals. As an active non-profit organization, it also has the mandate and institutional structure to train and engage students over the long term, even as students come in and out of the program. Again, this demonstrates how organizations and groups seeking to participate in long-term settlement work benefit from institutional support.

And what of the small, community-based groups that sprang up in the aftermath of Alan Kurdi's death in 2015? What do they need to continue their settlement work in the long term? In Pictou County, Nova Scotia, a group of residents from a variety of backgrounds formed a group called Safe Harbour in response to the events in late 2015. Though secular, in the beginning Safe Harbour established a close working partnership with Trinity United Church, which was connected to a national SAH and had members with experience sponsoring during the Southeast Asian refugee movement. Safe Harbour is still sponsoring today. A group of approximately thirty volunteers assists in providing settlement support to over forty-seven newcomers from Syria and a variety of other countries. This has likely been possible because, in 2018, the group secured private funding to hire a full-time newcomer service coordinator. Their coordinator, Kailee Brennan, oversees the recruitment and training of volunteers by getting their police checks; matching them with tasks; keeping them engaged and connected with the group and its mission; posting to social media; ensuring protection of confidentiality and privacy; coordinating sponsorship applications, arrivals, and settlement; and more.

When we spoke with Kailee, she stressed just how much work managing such a group can be: "It's really helpful to have a coordinator that is matching them to tasks, checking in on them, taking things off their plate. It helps to have a driving force whose sole purpose is to maintain momentum. It's become a full-time job in our scenario." Importantly, having this kind of support has allowed the group to continue fostering partnerships with a network of organizations. Recently, Safe Harbour began working with private partners (The Shapiro Foundation, Talent Beyond Boundaries, RefugePoint, Glen Haven Manor, and local employers experiencing labour shortages) to focus on complementary pathways for resettlement, especially through Canada's Economic Mobility Pathways Pilot program for the economic migration of skilled refugees. This kind of migration does not happen very quickly, but local employers have committed to providing fifteen job offers for refugees resettled in Pictou County over the next five years. Such private partnerships have allowed this small group to flourish past the Syrian Initiative; still, Safe Harbour's funding is only guaranteed until 2025.

It should be noted that the structural components that have been developed in each of the previously mentioned groups might not be possible or desirable for many smaller, more ad hoc sponsorship and settlement volunteer groups. This is where organizations like the Catholic Centre for Immigrants (CCI) or other local organizations like Ottawa Community Immigrant Services Organization (OCISO) can play a vital role. When adequately funded, these organizations can lighten the load placed on community groups. We saw in previous chapters how the CCI's institutional capacity fostered the ROC's engagement over the years; surely other faith-based and secular volunteer groups could be similarly supported in the long term.

The corporate world can also play a role in financing settlement and sponsorship work. Businesses have generally been engaged as donors and partners for settlement organizations and private sponsors. There are bound to be more innovative ways the private sector can become involved in settlement. In one unique circumstance during the Syrian Initiative, a Toronto-based investment firm, Donville Kent Asset Management, decided to privately sponsor a Syrian refugee family (CTV 2015). More recently, a number of corporate partners have collaborated with UNHCR Canada and national non-profit organizations to workshop ways in which all sectors can contribute to resettlement—and to the work of integration, networking, certification, and job-finding that is involved with this (Accenture 2020). The corporate avenue will be increasingly important in years to come since the UNHCR and global partners have declared their intention—in the Global Compact on Refugees and corresponding Comprehensive Refugee Response Framework—to seek not only to increase resettlement numbers but also to strengthen complementary pathways for refuge-seekers through education, labour, and other immigration streams (UNHCR 2019b).

In 2018, Lifeline Syria, a refugee sponsorship organization based in Toronto, began a partnership with Cisco—a multinational tech company—and NPower Canada—a charitable organization that guides underserved young adults into meaningful careers—to launch

Syrian refugees aged eighteen to twenty-nine into digital careers (Lifeline Syria 2019). As part of the partnership, NPower Canada offers a fifteen-week workforce development program at no cost and then helps with job placement.

The above examples indicate that various secular groups are gaining credibility and legitimacy within the settlement sector and with the federal government. They have each tapped into particular assets, cultural competences, and interests within the Canadian community at large to develop so-far sustainable, long-term volunteer networks. They have played an important role in shaping government policy, including by increasing quotas for LGBTQ+, Yazidi, and Syrian refugees in recent years. They have also been increasingly supported and funded by the government and treated as partners in settlement. Governments can continue this support both financially and by extending the policies and quotas that have long enabled faith-based communities to participate in settlement work.

Lisa Hébert from CRR values the contribution from churches, who have been vital to the growth of refugee sponsorship: "We've learned so much from them and we're grateful for what has been passed on." Ottawa's faith communities have been important partners in mentoring groups new to settlement work. As SAHs, they have acted as guarantors, trainers, and more for many nascent sponsorship groups across the country. CRR itself has partnered with a faith-based SAH, the Canadian Unitarian Council, based in Toronto. And CRR initially learned from manuals put together by congregations on best practices in sponsorship. Still, Hébert acknowledges that the system is set up to work best for faith-based organizations, since it was designed *for* and *by* them in the first place.

One particular problem for secular or nascent sponsor groups is the limited number of sponsorships SAHs can undertake each year. Caps were imposed in 2012 by the Harper government to help reduce application inventories as wait times for private sponsorships soared (RSTP 2015). Though inventories have been somewhat reduced today, and the annual cap for SAH applications is increasing every year, the 2020 cap was set at 12,500 (IRCC 2020c). SAHs face a significant internal and external pressure to share their quotas. Given the historic homophobia within some faith-based institutions, Hébert says CRR is grateful that their Rainbow Coalition 4 Refuge successfully lobbied the federal government to make the Rainbow Refugee Assistance Partnership a regular, ongoing program. This was an important gain, which was secured recently, and demonstrates a commitment within Canada to support LGBTQ+ sponsorships.

* * *

It is often said that a small group of thoughtful, committed individuals can change the world.[2] Our hope is that the stories of the people in this book have shown how true this maxim is. From Ottawa's involvement in the national response to the large-scale displacement of Southeast Asians to the ROC's humble beginnings in 1990 to sanctuary and Syrian resettlement, we have seen how time, compassion, and commitment gradually became expertise and credibility, how relationships between refuge-seekers and residents fuelled changes in law and policy, and how everyday choices by ordinary people have been the bedrock of Canada's ability to resettle hundreds of thousands of refuge-seekers over the last half century. As Louisa Taylor puts it: "The whole world is paying attention to refugees now, so what we do now can help people understand that helping people who have left their homes is actually part of Canadian values."

During our many conversations, ROC members insisted that we make it clear that they gained far more from their involvement than they gave—they learned to see refugees as people simply in need of refuge and friendship. These friendships turned members' zeal into lasting passion for settlement work as they learned through experience just how deeply reciprocal and enriching it could be. Radamis Zaky, a PhD candidate at the University of Ottawa from Egypt, shared a story that perfectly demonstrates this. In 2014, a few years after his arrival in Ottawa and also a few years after he had started attending St. Joe's Parish, he tentatively approached the ROC to ask for their assistance. Radamis had a friend, a refugee claimant, who he felt needed some community support. However, Radamis hesitated to approach the ROC because he worried that the Catholic group might not be keen on helping his friend, a Muslim. To his surprise, the members were very enthusiastic. He remembers that they went to visit his friend immediately. A few months later, when the man's wife and children were able to join him in Canada, the ROC continued to provide friendship to the whole family. Reflecting on this, Radamis (who

---

2   This quotation is typically attributed to anthropologist Margaret Mead, though we could not find a direct citation for it.

has since joined the ROC) said, "And they do this because they really want to do this; not because of some superior, colonial idea that 'we' as white people will save these refugees ... but no, they went to have supper with this family just to make them feel safe."

Friendship between members has certainly been another key to the ROC's sustainability over the years. Friendship encouraged and enlivened Committee members. The ROC members respected each other, celebrated successes and holidays together, and genuinely appreciated the community they had become a part of. John Weir spoke of the ROC's admiration for their founder, Louise: "A lot of people are in this committee because of her legacy and the respect that we have for her, and what she has accomplished. And we don't want that to be lost." Robyne Warren told us: "I am so proud to be a part of the ROC.... I have friends for life."

Friends drew each other into the work. And friendships have kept the ROC going till today. Louise Lalonde invited Margo Gauthier; Connie Goulet invited Robyne Warren; Pierre Gauthier invited Radamis Zaky; and then they invited us to write this book. Now as we finish sharing their story, we invite you to this work, the work of making a place for those seeking refuge all around us—whether it be someone halfway around the world or someone living next door. The ordinary actions you choose today can amount to something extraordinary.

References

Abella, Irving M., and Harold Martin Troper. 2017. *None Is Too Many: Canada and the Jews of Europe, 1933–1948*. Toronto: University of Toronto Press.

Accenture. 2020. "How Corporate Canada Can Play a Role in Refugee Resettlement." Accenture. April 13, 2020. YouTube video, 4:40. https://www.youtube.com/watch?v=s2tnMrcZ7Vo&ab_channel=Accenture.

Adler-Nissen, Rebecca, Katrine Emilie Andersen, and Lene Hansen. 2020. "Images, Emotions, and International Politics: The Death of Alan Kurdi." *Review of International Studies* 46(1): 75–95.

Amuedo-Dorantes, Catalina, Cynthia Bansak, and Susan Pozo. 2021. "Refugee Admissions and Public Safety: Are Refugee Settlement Areas More Prone to Crime?" *International Migration Review* 55(1): 135–165.

Anderson, Christopher, and Dagmar Soennecken. 2018. "Taking the Harper Government's Refugee Policy to Court." In *Policy Change, Courts and the Canadian Constitution*, edited by Emmett McFarlane, 290–312. Toronto: University of Toronto Press. https://yorkspace.library.yorku.ca/xmlui/handle/10315/37154?show=full.

Angus Reid Institute. 2015. "Canadians Divided along Political Lines over Whether to Accept Thousands of Refugees in Current Crisis." News release, September 4, 2015. https://angusreid.org/refugee-crisis/.

Armstrong, Jane. 2007. "Iranian Refugee Awaits Fate behind Bars as His Call to Police Breached Sanctuary." *Globe and Mail*, February 19, 2007. https://www.theglobeandmail.com/news/national/iranian-refugee-awaits-fate-behind-bars-as-his-call-to-police-breached-sanctuary/article1353621/.

Atak, Idil, Graham Hudson, and Delphine Nakache. 2018. "The Securitisation of Canada's Refugee System: Reviewing the Unintended Consequences of the 2012 Reform." *Refugee Survey Quarterly* 37(1): 1–24.

Aylesworth, Laurence S., and Peter G. Ossorio. 1983. "Refugees: Cultural Displacement and Its Effects." *Advances in Descriptive Psychology* 3:45–93.

Baudoin, Martha. 1981. "The Religious of the Sacred Heart in Canada 1842–1980." *CCHA Study Sessions* 48:43–60. http://www.cchahistory.ca/journal/CCHA1981/Baudoin.pdf.

Berthiaume, Lee. 2015. "Few Ethnic Minorities among Syrians Sponsored by Canadian Government." *Ottawa Citizen*, September 22, 2015. https://

ottawacitizen.com/news/politics/few-ethnic-minorities-among-syrians
-sponsored-by-canadian-government.

Bier, David J. 2021. "Biden Tells the State Department to Launch Private Refugee
Sponsorship." Cato Institute. February 5, 2021. https://www.cato.org/blog
/biden-tells-state-department-launch-private-refugee-sponsorship.

Blain, Marie-Jeanne, Lourdes Rodriguez del Barrio, Roxane Caron, Marie-
Claire Rufagari, Myriam Richard, Yannick Boucher, and Caroline Lester.
2019. "Expériences de parrainage collectif de personnes réfugiées au
Québec : Perspectives de parrains et de personnes réfugiées de la Syrie."
Lien social et Politiques 88:204–229.

Bond, Jennifer. 2016. "The Defence of Duress in Canadian Refugee Law."
Queen's Law Journal 41(2): 409–454.

Bond, Jennifer, Nathan Benson, and Jared Porter. 2020. "Guilt by Association:
Ezokola's Unfinished Business in Canadian Refugee Law." *Refugee
Survey Quarterly* 39:1–25.

Bond, Jennifer, and Ania Kwadrans. 2019. "Resettling Refugees through
Community Sponsorship: A Revolutionary Operational Approach Built
on Traditional Legal Infrastructure." *Refuge: Canada's Journal on Refugees*
35(2): 87–109.

Bramadat, Paul. 2014. "Don't Ask, Don't Tell: Refugee Settlement and Religion
in British Columbia." *Journal of the American Academy of Religion* 82(4):
907–937.

Brownlee, Kimberley. 2017. "Civil Disobedience." In *Stanford Encyclopedia of
Philosophy,* edited by Edward N. Zalta. Stanford University: Metaphysics
Research Lab. https://plato.stanford.edu/entries/civil-disobedience/.

Byrne, Terry. 2007. *Where the Spirit Lives: A History of St. Joseph's Parish, 1856–
2006.* Ottawa: St. Joseph's Parish. http://www.st-josephs.ca/about
/history/where-the-spirit-lives-by-terry-byrne-2/.

Cameron, Geoffrey. 2020. "Reluctant Partnerships: A Political History of Private
Sponsorship in Canada (1947–1980)." In *Strangers to Neighbours: Refugee
Sponsorship in Context,* edited by Shauna Labman and Geoffrey Cameron,
19–41. Montreal and Kingston: McGill-Queen's University Press.

———. 2021. *Send them Here: Religion, Politics, and Refugee Resettlement in
North America.* Montreal and Kingston: McGill-Queen's University
Press.

Canadian Ethnic Studies. 2018. "Special Issue: Canada's Syrian Refugee Program,
Intergroup Relationships and Identities." *Canadian Ethnic Studies* 50(2).

Carrière, April. 2016. *History and Legacy of Refugee Resettlement in Ottawa: A
Primer.* Ottawa Local Immigration Partnership (OLIP). http://cciottawa
.ca/wp-content/uploads/Myths-History-and-Stats.pdf.

Carver, Peter. 2016. "A Failed Discourse of Distrust Amid Significant
Procedural Change: The Harper Government's Legacy in Immigration
and Refugee Law." *Revue d'études constitutionnelles* 21:209–234.

CBC. 2004. "Man Claiming Sanctuary Given OK to Leave Church." News release, December 13, 2004. https://www.cbc.ca/news/canada/man -claiming-sanctuary-given-ok-to-leave-church-1.506356.

———. 2005. "The Church as Sanctuary." News release, February 14, 2005. https://www.cbc.ca/news2/background/immigration/sanctuary.html.

———. 2007. "Refugee Free after 21 Months in Ottawa Church." News release, October 3, 2007. https://www.cbc.ca/news/canada/ottawa/refugee-free -after-21-months-hiding-in-ottawa-church-1.654737.

CCR (Canadian Council for Refugees). 2008. *Support Bill C-280 Calling for the Implementation of the Refugee Appeal Division.* https://ccrweb.ca/sites /ccrweb.ca/files/static-files/documents/meetingRADsenate.pdf.

———. 2012. *The Experience of Refugee Claimants at Refugee Hearings at the Immigration and Refugee Board.* Report, January 2012. https://ccrweb.ca /sites/ccrweb.ca/files/irb_hearings_report_final.pdf.

———. 2014 *Canada's Private Sponsorship of Refugees Program: Proud History, Uncertain Future.* Canadian Council for Refugees. Report, December 2014. https://ccrweb.ca/en/private-sponsorship-refugees-proud-history -uncertain-future.

———. 2017. "2017 Immigration Levels: Comments." Accessed June 2021. https://ccrweb.ca/en/2017-immigration-levels-comments.

———. 2021. "Federal Court of Appeal Decision Disappointing but Acknowledges Ineffectiveness of Review Process." Media release, April 15, 2021. https:// ccrweb.ca/en/federal-court-appeal-decision-disappointing.

———. n.d. "Refugee Appeal Division: Frequently Asked Questions." Accessed November 23, 2020. https://ccrweb.ca/sites/ccrweb.ca/files /static-files/RADpage/PAGE0003.HTM.

Chapman, Ashley. 2014. *Private Sponsorship and Public Policy: Political Barriers to Church-Connected Refugee Resettlement in Canada.* Citizens for Public Justice. Report, September 2014. https://cpj.ca/wp-content/uploads/ PrivateSponsorshipandPublicPolicyReport-1.pdf.

Chase, Steven, Daniel Leblanc, Mark Mackinnon, and Campbell Clark. 2015. "Canada's Refugee Resettlement Plan Remains a Work in Progress." *Globe and Mail,* November 25, 2015. https://www.theglobeandmail.com /news/politics/canadas-refugee-resettlement-plan-remains-a-work-in -progress/article27488307/.

CIMM (House of Commons Standing Committee on Citizenship and Immigration). 2006a. "Evidence." House of Commons Standing Committee on Citizenship and Immigration, 39th Parliament, 1st Session, No. 22, November 2, 2006. https://www.ourcommons.ca/Document Viewer/en/39-1/CIMM/meeting-22/evidence#T0920.

———. 2006b. "Evidence." House of Commons Standing Committee on Citizenship and Immigration, 39th Parliament, 1st Session, No. 16, October 3, 2006. https://www.ourcommons.ca/DocumentViewer/en/39-1 /CIMM/meeting-17/evidence.

———. 2006c. "Minutes." House of Commons Standing Committee on Citizenship and Immigration, 39th Parliament, 1st Session, No. 22, November 2, 2006. https://www.ourcommons.ca/DocumentViewer/en /39-1/CIMM/meeting-22/minutes.

———. 2007a. "Safeguarding Asylum: Sustaining Canada's Commitments to Refugees." House of Commons Standing Committee on Citizenship and Immigration, May 2007. https://www.ourcommons.ca/Content /Committee/391/CIMM/Reports/RP2969755/cimmrp15/cimmrp15-e.pdf.

———. 2007b. "Evidence." House of Commons Standing Committee on Citizenship and Immigration, 39th Parliament, 1st Session, No. 34, February 13, 2007. https://www.ourcommons.ca/DocumentViewer/en /39-1/CIMM/meeting-34/evidence.

———. 2008. "Evidence." House of Commons Standing Committee on Citizenship and Immigration, 39th Parliament, 2nd Session, No. 45, May 14, 2008. https://www.ourcommons.ca/DocumentViewer/en/39-2 /CIMM/meeting-45/evidence.

City of Ottawa. 2015. "City Mobilizes to Help Refugees of Syrian Crisis: Mayor Jim Watson Launches Refugee 613, United for Refugees at Public Forum." News release, October 1, 2015. https://ottawa.ca/en/news /city-mobilizes-help-refugees-syrian-crisis-mayor-jim-watson-launches -refugee-613-united-refugees-public-forum.

Clark, Campbell. 2002. "Coderre to Delay Plan for Refugee Appeal Division." *Globe and Mail*, April 29, 2002. https://www.theglobeandmail.com /news/national/coderre-to-delay-plan-for-refugee-appeal-division /article4134434/.

Clarke, Juanne Nancarrow, and Taylor Marlow. 2020. "The Cracks in Our Admired Private Refugee Sponsorship Program." *Policy Options/ Options Politiques* (Institute for Research on Public Policy), January 30, 2020. https://policyoptions.irpp.org/magazines/january-2020/the-cracks -in-our-admired-private-refugee-sponsorship-program/.

Cohen, Juliet. 2001. "Errors of Recall and Credibility: Can Omissions and Discrepancies in Successive Statements Reasonably Be Said to Undermine Credibility of Testimony?" *Medico-Legal Journal* 69(1): 25–34.

CPC (Conservative Party of Canada). 2021. *Canada's Recovery Plan*. Conservative Party of Canada. Summer 2021. https://cpcassets.conservative.ca/wp -content/uploads/2021/09/08200659/e4cd8c0115c3ea0.pdf/.

Croft, Dave. 2018. "Yukon Cares Ups Efforts to Bring More Syrian Refugees to Territory." CBC News. January 15, 2018. https://www.cbc.ca/news /canada/north/yukon-cares-refugees-syria-1.4488107.

CTV. 2015. "Toronto Investment Firm to Privately Sponsor Syrian Refugee Family." CTV News. September 13, 2015. https://www.ctvnews.ca/canada /toronto-investment-firm-to-privately-sponsor-syrian-refugee-family -1.2561136.

Cunningham, Hilary. 2012. "The Emergence of the Ontario Sanctuary Coalition: From Humanitarian and Compassionate Review to Civil Initiative." In *Sanctuary Practices in International Perspectives: Migration, Citizenship and Social Movements*, edited by Randy Lippert and Sean Rehaag, 162–174. Abingdon: Routledge.

Denton, Thomas. 2016. "Refugee Program Good in Theory, Flawed in Practice." *Winnipeg Free Press*, September 21, 2016. https://www. winnipegfreepress.com/opinion/analysis/refugee-program-good-in -theory-flawed-in-practice-394230361.html.

Enns, Thea, Luann Good Gingrich, and Kaylee Perez. 2020. "Religious Heritage, Institutionalized Ethos, and Synergies: The Mennonite Central Committee and Canada's Private Sponsorship of Refugees Program." In *Strangers to Neighbours: Refugee Sponsorship in Context*, edited by Shauna Labman and Geoffrey Cameron, 95–111. Montreal and Kingston: McGill-Queen's University Press.

Environics. 2020. *Focus Canada 2020 - Fall 2020: Canadian Public Opinion about Immigration and Refugees - Final Report*. The Environics Institute for Survey Research. Report, October 7, 2020. https://www.environics institute.org/docs/default-source/project-documents/fc-fall-2020 ---immigration/focus-canada-fall-2020---public-opinion-on -immigration-refugees---final-report.pdf?sfvrsn=bd51588f_2.

——. 2021. *Private Refugee Sponsorship in Canada*. The Environics Institute for Survey Research and Refugee 613. Projects, Project details, June 17, 2021. https://www.environicsinstitute.org/projects/project-details/private -refugee-sponsorship-in-canada---2021-market-study?fbclid=IwAR0ky cGgTunlL3xqICSvilkeW1UZ1xV29eXTnBmY6ff0R1WJqWeVqkvTJKI.

Evans Cameron, Hilary. 2010. "Refugee Status Determinations and the Limits of Memory." *International Journal of Refugee Law* 22(4): 469–511.

Fraser Institute. 2017. "Generosity in Canada and the United States: The 2017 Generosity Index." News release, December 13, 2017. https://www .fraserinstitute.org/studies/generosity-in-canada-and-the-united-states -the-2017-generosity-index.

Globe and Mail. 2015. "The Refugee Crisis: Four Things to Know Before You Vote." *Globe and Mail*. September 15, 2015. https://www.theglobeandmail. com/news/politics/canada-and-the-refugee-crisis-four-things-to -know-before-youvote/article26363975/.

Goodyear, Sheena. 2015. "Syrian Refugees Not Always Available for Sponsorship, Canadians Learn." CBC News. December 23, 2015. https:// www.cbc.ca/news/canada/refugee-sponsors-non-syrians-1.3376790.

Gorham, Deborah. 2016. *Marion Dewar: A Life of Action*. Toronto: Second Story Press.

Gouthro, Patricia A. 2010. *Grassroots and Governance: Exploring Informal Learning Opportunities to Support Active Citizenship and Community-Based*

Organizations within Canada. Canadian Council on Learning. http://
  en.copian.ca/library/research/ccl/grassroots_governance/grassroots
  _governance.pdf.
Government of Canada. 2018. *Government Response to the Report of the House of
  Commons Standing Committee on Citizenship and Immigration Entitled: Road to
  Recovery: Resettlement Issues for Yazidi Women and Children in Canada.* https://
  www.ourcommons.ca/content/Committee/421/CIMM/GovResponse
  /RP10007620/421_CIMM_Rpt18_GR/421_CIMM_Rpt18_GR-e.pdf.
———. 2020a. "CIMM - Humanitarian and Compassionate Considerations."
  Last modified September 18, 2020. https://www.canada.ca/en/immigration
  -refugees-citizenship/corporate/transparency/committees/march
  -12-2020/humanitarian-and-compassionate-considerations.html#shr-pg0.
———. 2020b. *2020 Annual Report to Parliament on Immigration.* https://www
  .canada.ca/en/immigration-refugees-citizenship/corporate/publications
  -manuals/annual-report-parliament-immigration-2020.html.
Grant, Angus, and Sean Rehaag. 2016. "Unappealing: An Assessment of the
  Limits on Appeal Rights in Canada's New Refugee Determination
  System." *Osgoode Legal Studies Research Paper Series* 132:1–48.
GRSI (Global Refugee Sponsorship Initiative). 2019. "Global Refugee
  Sponsorship Initiative: At A Glance." *Global Refugee Sponsorship
  Initiative* 19:1–2. https://refugeesponsorship.org/_uploads/5cc7356402392.
  pdf.
———.n.d. "Global Refugee Sponsorship Initiative." Accessed June 2021.
  https://refugeesponsorship.org/.
Hamilton, Leah K., Luisa Veronis, and Margaret Walton-Roberts, eds. 2020. *A
  National Project: Syrian Refugee Resettlement in Canada.* Montreal and
  Kingston: McGill-Queen's University Press.
Hicks, Jeff. 2016. "McCallum under Pressure to Bring in More Refugees." *The
  Record*, July 14, 2016. https://www.therecord.com/news/waterloo-region
  /2016/07/14/mccallum-under-pressure-to-bring-in-more-refugees.
  html.
Hersh, Nicholas. 2015. "Challenges to Assessing Same-Sex Relationships
  under Refugee Law in Canada." *McGill Law Journal* 60(3): 527–571.
House of Commons. 2005. "House Publications: Debates." House of
  Commons, 38th Parliament, 1st Session, Vol. 140, No. 159, November 28,
  2005. https://www.ourcommons.ca/DocumentViewer/en/38-1/house
  /sitting-159/hansard.
———. 2006. "House Publications: Debates." House of Commons, 39th
  Parliament, 1st Session, Vol. 141, No. 022, May 12, 2006. https://www
  .ourcommons.ca/DocumentViewer/en/39-1/house/sitting-22/hansard.
———. 2007a. "House Publications: Debates." House of Commons, 39th
  Parliament, 1st Session, Vol. 141, No. 098, January 29, 2007. https://www
  .ourcommons.ca/DocumentViewer/en/39-1/house/sitting-98/hansard.

———. 2007b. "House Publications: Debates." House of Commons, 39th Parliament, 1st Session, Vol. 141, No. 125, March 21, 2007. https://www.ourcommons.ca/DocumentViewer/en/39-1/house/sitting-125/hansard#OOB-1969149.

———. 2007c. "Vote No. 193." House of Commons, 39th Parliament, 1st Session, Vote No. 193, May 30, 2007. https://www.ourcommons.ca/Members/en/votes/39/1/193?view=result.

———. 2009. "Vote No. 157." House of Commons, 40th Parliament, 2nd Session, Vote No. 157, December 10, 2009. https://www.ourcommons.ca/Members/en/votes/40/2/157?view=party.

———. 2010. "Debates." House of Commons, 40th Parliament, 3rd Session, Vol. 145, No. 020, March 30, 2010. https://www.ourcommons.ca/DocumentViewer/en/40-3/house/sitting-20/hansard.

———. n.d. "Our Procedure: Legislative Process." House of Commons. Accessed June 2020. https://www.ourcommons.ca/About/OurProcedure/LegislativeProcess/c_g_legislativeprocess-e.htm.

Human Rights Watch. 2001. "The New Racism: The Political Manipulation of Ethnicity in Cote d'Ivoire." News release, August 28, 2001. https://www.hrw.org/report/2001/08/28/new-racism/political-manipulation-ethnicity-cote-divoire.

Hyndman, Jennifer, William Payne, and Shauna Jimenez. 2016. *The State of Private Refugee Sponsorship in Canada: Trends, Issues, and Impacts.* Refugee Research Network and Centre for Refugee Studies Policy Brief, submitted to the Government of Canada. https://refugeeresearch.net/wp-content/uploads/2017/02/hyndman_feb%E2%80%9917.pdf.

IRCC (Immigration, Refugees and Citizenship Canada). 2008. "Formative Evaluation of the Pre-Removal Risk Assessment Program". Immigration, Refugees and Citizenship. Last modified June 26, 2009. https://www.canada.ca/en/immigration-refugees-citizenship/corporate/reports-statistics/evaluations/removal-risk-assessment-program/section-4.html

———. 2011. "Evaluation of the Host Program." Immigration, Refugees and Citizenship. Last modified December 28, 2011. https://www.canada.ca/en/immigration-refugees-citizenship/corporate/reports-statistics/evaluations/host-program.html.

———. 2012a. "Changes to the Pre-Removal Risk Assessment Program under the New Legislation." Immigration, Refugees and Citizenship Canada, Evaluation Division. Last modified December 17, 2012. https://www.canada.ca/en/immigration-refugees-citizenship/corporate/publications-manuals/operational-bulletins-manuals/bulletins-2012/440-december-17-2012.html.

———. 2012b. "Regulations Amending the Immigration and Refugee Protection Regulations." Last modified October 18, 2012. https://canadagazette.gc.ca/rp-pr/p2/2012/2012-11-07/html/sor-dors225-eng.html.

———. 2015. "Canada Offers Leadership on the Syrian Refugee Crisis." News release, November 24, 2015. https://www.canada.ca/en/immigration -refugees-citizenship/news/2015/11/canada-offers-leadership-on-the -syrian-refugee-crisis.html.

———. 2019. "Canada Introduces New Initiative to Support LGBTQ2 Refugees." News release, June 1, 2019. https://www.canada.ca/en /immigration-refugees-citizenship/news/2019/06/canada-announces -new-initiative-to-support-lgbtq2-refugees.html.

———. 2020a. "Canada - Admissions of Resettled Refugees by Country of Citizenship and Immigration Category." Accessed June 2020. https:// open.canada.ca/data/en/dataset/4a1b260a-7ac4-4985-80a0-603 bfe4aec11.

———. 2020b. "Supplementary Information for the 2021-2023 Immigration Levels Plan." Last modified June 18, 2021. https://www.canada.ca/en /immigration-refugees-citizenship/news/notices/supplementary -immigration-levels-2021-2023.html.

———. 2020c. "Supplementary Information 2020-2022 Immigration Levels Plan." Last modified March 12, 2020. https://www.canada.ca/en /immigration-refugees-citizenship/news/notices/supplementary -immigration-levels-2020.html.

John Paul II. 1990. "Message of His Holiness John Paul II for Lent 1990, encyclical letters." Vatican website. Accessed June 2021. http://www .vatican.va/content/john-paul-ii/en/messages/lent/documents/hf_jp-ii _mes_19890908_lent-1990.html.

Johnson, Claudia. 1970. *A White House Diary*. Austin: University of Texas Press.

Kaduuli, Stephen. 2020. *Continuing Welcome: A Progress Report on A Half Welcome*. Citizens for Public Justice. Report, June 2020. https://cpj.ca /report/continuing-welcome/.

Kaida, Lisa, Feng Hou, and Max Stick. 2020. "The Long-Term Economic Outcomes of Refugee Private Sponsorship." Immigration, Refugees and Citizenship Canada. Last modified January 13, 2020. https:// www150.statcan.gc.ca/n1/pub/11f0019m/11f0019m2019021-eng.htm.

Keung, Nicholas. 2019. "Sponsoring Refugees Called a 'Win-Win' for Workplaces." *Toronto Star*, July 1, 2019. https://www.thestar.com/news /gta/2019/07/01/sponsoring-refugees-called-a-win-win-for-workplaces. html.

———. 2021. "'We Have Done It Before and We Can Do It Again': Organizers Who Helped Resettle Syrian Refugees Launch New Campaign amid Afghan Crisis." *Toronto Star*, August 31, 2021. https://www.thestar.com /news/canada/2021/08/31/we-have-done-it-before-and-we-can-do-it -again-organizers-who-helped-resettle-syrian-refugees-launch-new -campaign-amid-afghan-crisis.html.

Kurdi, Tima. 2018. *The Boy on the Beach: My Family's Escape from Syria and Our Hope for a New Home*. New York: Simon & Schuster.

Kyriakides, Christopher, Lubna Bajjali, Arthur McLuhan, and Karen Anderson. 2018. "Beyond Refuge: Contested Orientalism and Persons of Self-Rescue." *Canadian Ethnic Studies* 50(2): 59–78.

Labman, Shauna. 2016. "Private Sponsorship: Complementary or Conflicting Interests?" *Refuge: Canada's Journal on Refugees* 32(1): 67–80.

———. 2019. *Crossing Law's Borders: Canada's Refugee Resettlement Program*. Vancouver: UBC Press.

Labman, Shauna, and Geoffrey Cameron, eds. 2020. *Strangers to Neighbours: Refugee Sponsorship in Context*. Montreal and Kingston: McGill-Queen's University Press.

Labman, Shauna, and Jennifer Hyndman. 2019. *BVOR Briefing*. Centre for Refugee Studies, York University. https://crs.info.yorku.ca/files/2019/04/BVOR-Briefing-2019-May1.pdf?x44358.

Laucius, Joanne. 2016. "About 150 Syrian Refugee Children Already in Ottawa Schools." *Ottawa Sun*, February 9, 2016. https://ottawasun.com/2016/02/09/about-150-syrian-refugee-children-already-in-ottawa-schools/wcm/cc0214ff-278f-4624-9b1d-9e86c091de9a.

LaViolette, Nicole. 2010. "Canada's Queer Community Needs to Help Persecuted Sexual Minorities." *Globe and Mail*, July 22, 2010. https://www.theglobeandmail.com/opinion/canadas-queer-community-needs-to-help-persecuted-sexual-minorities/article1212554/.

———. 2014. "Sexual Orientation, Gender Identity, and the Refugee Determination Process in Canada." *Journal of Research in Gender Studies* 4(2): 68–123.

Lenard, Patti Tamara. 2020. "How Should We Think about Private Sponsorship of Refugees?" In *Strangers to Neighbours: Refugee Sponsorship in Context*, edited by Shauna Labman and Geoffrey Cameron, 61–73. Montreal and Kingston: McGill-Queen's University Press.

———. 2021. "How Exceptional? Welcoming Refugees the Canadian Way." *American Review of Canadian Studies* 51(1): 78–94.

Lenard, Patti Tamara, and Terry Macdonald. 2019. "Democracy Versus Security as Standards of Political Legitimacy: The Case of National Policy on Irregular Migrant Arrivals." *Perspectives on Politics* 49(2): 371–387.

Levitz, Stephanie. 2015. "Does Canada's Refugee Policy Discriminate against Syrian Muslims?" CTV News. January 15, 2015. https://www.ctvnews.ca/canada/does-canada-s-refugee-policy-discriminate-against-syrian-muslims-1.2189947.

Library of Parliament. 2010. "Legislative Summary of Bill C-11: An Act to Amend the Immigration and Refugee Protection Act and the Federal Courts Act (Balanced Refugee Reform Act)." Library of Parliament, Research Publications. Last modified May 12, 2010. https://lop.parl.ca

/sites/PublicWebsite/default/en_CA/ResearchPublications/Legislative Summaries/403C11E#a2p2p3p3.

Lifeline Syria. 2019. "Cisco Canada Partners with Lifeline Syria and NPower Canada to Help Syrian Newcomers Thrive in Technology Sector." News release, June 24, 2019. http://lifelinesyria.ca/cisco-canada-partners -with-lifeline-syria-and-npower-canada-to-help-syrian-newcomers -thrive-in-technology-sector/.

Lindsay, Bethany. 2018. "Philanthropists Donate $3.5M to Help Bring Almost 700 Refugees to Canada." CBC News. November 14, 2018. https://www. cbc.ca/news/canada/british-columbia/donations-help-bring-hundreds -refugees-canada-1.4904331.

Lippert, Randy. 2005a. "Rethinking Sanctuary: The Canadian Context, 1983– 2003." *International Migration Review* 39(2): 381–406.

———. 2005b. *Sanctuary, Sovereignty, Sacrifice: Canadian Sanctuary Incidents, Power, and Law.* Vancouver: UBC Press.

———. 2009. "Wither Sanctuary?" *Refuge* 26(1): 57–67.

Macklin, Audrey. 2009. "Refugee Roulette in the Canadian Casino." In *Refugee Roulette: Disparities in Asylum Adjudication and Proposals for Reform,* edited by Jaya Ramji-Nogales, Andrew I. Schoenholtz and Philip G. Schrag, 146–147. New York: NYU Press.

———. 2021. "Working against and with the State: From Sanctuary to Resettlement." *Migration and Society: Advances in Research* 4:31–46.

Macklin, Audrey, Kathryn Barber, Luin Goldring, Jennifer Hyndman, Anna Korteweg, Shauna Labman, and Jona Zyfi. 2018. "A Preliminary Investigation into Private Refugee Sponsors." *Canadian Ethnic Studies Journal* 50(2): 35–57.

Madokoro, Laura. 2017. "'Belated Signing': Race-Thinking and Canada's Approach to the 1951 Convention Relating to the Status of Refugees." In *Dominion of Race: Rethinking Canada's International History,* edited by Laura Madokoro, David Meren, and Francine McKenzie, 160–182. Vancouver: UBC Press.

———. 2018. "A Decade of Change: Refugee Movements from the Global South and the Transformation of Canada's Immigration Framework." In *Canada and the Third World: Overlapping Histories,* edited by Karen Dubinsky, Sean Mills, and Scott Rutherford, 217–245. Toronto: University of Toronto Press.

Manzanedo, Cristina. 2019. *Community-Based Sponsorship in Spain: What Are the Experiences?* Friedrich Ebert Stiftung. Regional Project, "Flight, Migration, Integration in Europe," July 2019. http://library.fes.de/pdf -files/bueros/budapest/15599.pdf.

Marshall, Kristin. 2014. "Offering Sanctuary to Failed Refugee Claimants in Canada." *Forced Migration Review* 1(48): 38.

Masterson, Daniel, and Vasil Yasenov. 2019. "Does Halting Refugee Resettle-
    ment Reduce Crime? Evidence from the United States Refugee Ban."
    Institute for the Study of Labour (IZA), Discussion Paper No. 12551.
McKinlay, Christine. 2008. "Welcoming the Stranger: The Canadian Church
    and the Private Sponsorship of Refugees Program." Dissertation.
    Toronto: Ryerson University.
Michels, David, and David Blaikie. 2009. "Religious Justification for the
    Practice of Ecclesiastical Sanctuary." In *Giving Sanctuary to Illegal
    Immigrants: Between Civil Disobedience and Legal Obligation*, edited by
    Lorraine Derocher. Sherbrooke, QC: La Revue de Droit de l'Université
    de Sherbrooke.
Mills, Stuart. 2016. "Ottawa Charity Opens Furniture Depot for Syrian
    Refugees." CBC News. February 23, 2016. https://www.cbc.ca/news
    /canada/ottawa/ottawa-refugee-furniture-depot-1.3460489.
Milner, James, and Gil Loescher. 2011. *Responding to Protracted Refugee
    Situations: Lessons from a Decade of Discussion*. Refugee Studies Centre,
    Forced Migration Policy Briefing 6. https://www.refworld.org/pdfid
    /4da83a682.pdf.
Molloy, Michael J., Peter Duschinsky, Kurt F. Jensen, and Robert J. Shalka.
    2017. *Running on Empty: Canada and the Indochinese Refugees, 1975-1980*.
    Montreal and Kingston: McGill-Queen's University Press.
Morris, Stéfanie, Patti Tamara Lenard, and Stacey Haugen. 2021. "Refugee
    Resettlement and Family Reunification." *Journal of Refugee Studies* 34(1):
    130–148.
Neuwirth, Gertrud, and Lynn Clark. 1981. "Indochinese Refugees in Canada:
    Sponsorship and Adjustment." *The International Migration Review* 15(1/2):
    131–140.
NFFN (Senate Standing Committee on National Finance). 2008. "Seventeenth
    Report." Senate of Canada Standing Committee on National Finance,
    39th Parliament, 2nd Session, June 12, 2008. https://sencanada.ca
    /Content/SEN/Committee/392/fina/rep/rep17jun08-e.htm.
OCISO (Ottawa Community Immigrant Services Organization). 2019. "40
    Years of OCISO: It All Started in the 70s." Accessed June 2020. https://
    ociso.org/campaigns/40-years-of-ociso-it-all-started-in-the-70s/.
Okafor, Obiora Chinedu. 2020. *Refugee Law after 9/11: Sanctuary and Security in
    Canada and the US*. Vancouver: UBC Press.
OLIP (Ottawa Local Immigration Partnership). 2017. *The Arrival and Settlement
    of Syrian Refugees in Ottawa: Systems Response, Lessons Learned, and
    Future Directions*. Ottawa Syrian Refugee Research Initiative, November
    2017. http://olip-plio.ca/wp-content/uploads/2017/11/Syria-Report-1.pdf.
OMI (Missionary Oblates of Mary Immaculate). 1991. *An Apology to the First
    Nations of Canada by the Oblate Conference of Canada*. https://www.

st-josephs.ca/wp/wp-content/uploads/2021/06/oblate_apology
_english.pdf.

O'Toole, Erin. 2020. "O'Toole: True Blue Leadership." Erin O'Toole (website).
Accessed August 2020. https://erinotoole.ca/.

Paperny, Anna Mehler. 2021. "Canada Taken to Court over COVID Policy
That Pushes Asylum-Seekers to U.S." *Reuters*, May 4, 2021. https://
www.reuters.com/world/americas/exclusive-canada-taken-court
-over-covid-policy-that-pushes-asylum-seekers-us-2021-05-04/.

Parliament of Canada. "Bill C-50: First Reading." https://parl.ca/Document
Viewer/en/39-2/bill/C-50/first-reading/page-119#2.

Pearlman, Madison. 2020. "Operation Ezra: A New Way Forward." In
Strangers to Neighbours: Refugee Sponsorship in Context, edited by Shauna
Labman and Geoffrey Cameron, 112–133. Montreal and Kingston: McGill-
Queen's University Press.

Plasterer, Robyn. 2010. "Investigating Integration: The Geographies of the
WUSC Student Refugee Program at the University of British Columbia."
Refuge: Canada's Journal on Refugees 27(1): 59–74.

Pope, Steven. 1987. "Sanctuary: The Legal Institution in England." *Seattle
University Law Review* 10(3): 677–697.

Powell, James. 2014. "Project 4000." *Today in Ottawa's History* (blog). October 3,
2014. https://todayinottawashistory.wordpress.com/2014/10/03/project
-4000/.

Quan, Douglas. 2015. "Churches, Community Groups across Canada Rally to
Resettle Syrian Refugees." *National Post*, July 2, 2015. https://
nationalpost.com/news/canada/churchescommunity-groups-across
-canada-rally-to-resettle-syrian-refugees.

Rapley, Elizabeth. 2004. "We Should Not Forget Our Immigration History."
Catholic Centre for Immigrants. http://cciottawa.ca/wp-content
/uploads/History-1.pdf.

Refuge. 1986. "First Report on the Host Programme: Pilot Projects in London,
Winnipeg and Regina." *Refuge: Canada's Journal on Refugees*. https://
refuge.journals.yorku.ca/index.php/refuge/article/view/21495/20170.

Refugee Hub. 2019. "Terms of the BVOR Fund." Last modified May 2, 2019.
https://www.vancouver.anglican.ca/df_media.

Rehaag, Sean. 2009. "Bordering on Legality: Canadian Church Sanctuary
and the Rule of Law." *Refuge: Canada's Journal on Refugees* 26(1): 43–56.

——. 2019. "2018 Refugee Claim Data and IRB Member Recognition Rates."
Canadian Council for Refugees (CCR). Last modified June 19, 2019.
https://ccrweb.ca/en/2018-refugee-claim-data.

Reynolds, Johanna, and Christina Clark-Kazak, eds. 2019. "Special Issue:
Private Sponsorship in Canada." *Refuge: Canada's Journal on Refugees*
35(2): 1–130. https://doi.org/10.25071/1920-7336.40707.

Reynolds, Johanna, and Jennifer Hyndman. 2015. "A Turn in Canadian Refugee Policy and Practice." *Journal of Diplomacy and International Relations* 16(2): 41–56.

RIDR (Senate Standing Committee on Human Rights). 2008. "Proceedings of the Standing Senate Committee on Human Rights: Evidence." 39th Parliament, 2nd Session, Issue 6, June 2, 2008. https://sencanada.ca/en/Content/SEN/Committee/392/huma/06eva-e.

Ritchie, Flyn. 2013. "Why Would I Not Support José?" Church for Vancouver (website). October 22, 2013. https://churchforvancouver.ca/why-would-i-not-support-jose/.

Ritchie, Genevieve. 2018. "Civil Society, the State, and Private Sponsorship: The Political Economy of Refugee Resettlement." *International Journal of Lifelong Education* 37(6): 663–675.

RSTP (Refugee Sponsorship Training Program). 2015. "Frequently Asked Questions on SAH Global Cap Allocation and Usage - 2015." Refugee Sponsorship Training Program, Annex A. http://www.rstp.ca/wp-content/uploads/2015/06/FAQ-on-Allocations-Turkey-Pilot-Project.pdf.

———. n.d. "LGBTI Refugee Sponsorship Pilot Project." Accessed October 2020. http://www.rstp.ca/en/special-initiatives/lgbti-refugee-sponsorship-pilot-project/.

Russo, Robert M. 2008. "Security, Securitization and Human Capital: The New Wave of Canadian Immigration Laws." *International Journal of Human and Social Sciences* 3(4): 587–596.

Senate of Canada. 2008a. "Journals of the Senate." Senate of Canada, 39th Parliament, 2nd Session, Issue 72, June 18, 2008. https://sencanada.ca/en/content/sen/chamber/392/journals/072jr_2008-06-18-e.

———. 2008b. "Debates of the Senate." Senate of Canada, 39th Parliament, 2nd Session, Issue 72, June 18, 2008. https://sencanada.ca/en/content/sen/chamber/392/debates/072db_2008-06-18-e?language=e#71.

Showler, Peter. 2006. *Refugee Sandwich: Stories of Exile and Asylum.* Montreal and Kingston: McGill-Queen's University Press.

Siddiqi, Sara, and Duncan Koerber. 2020. "The Anatomy of a National Crisis: The Canadian Federal Government's Response to the 2015 Kurdi Refugee Case." *Canadian Journal of Communication* 45(3). https://doi.org/10.22230/cjc.2020v45n3a3585.

Small, David. 2018. *Mauril and Me, Testimonies to a Legacy; Mauril et moi, témoins d'un héritage.* Ottawa: Library and Archives Canada.

Smith, Craig Damian. 2020. "A Model for the World? Policy Transfer Theory and the Challenge of 'Exporting' Private Sponsorship to Europe." In *Strangers to Neighbours: Refugee Sponsorship in Context,* edited by Shauna Labman and Geoffrey Cameron, 286–302. Montreal and Kingston: McGill-Queen's University Press.

St. Joseph's Parish. 2021. "Question and Answer: Indian Residential Schools and the Missionary Oblates of Mary Immaculate." Last modified June 4, 2021. https://www.st-josephs.ca/questions-answers-indian-residential-schools -and-the-missionary-oblates-of-mary-immaculate/#more-18309.

Statistics Canada. 2016. "Canadian Demographics at a Glance: Second Edition." Statistics Canada, Demography Division. Last modified February 19, 2016. https://www150.statcan.gc.ca/n1/pub/91-003-x/2014001/section03/33-eng.htm.

The Canadian. 2021. "O'Toole Wants to 'Privatize' Refugee Sponsorship." *The Canadian*, August 25, 2021. https://thecanadian.news/2021/08/25 /otoole-wants-to-privatize-refugee-sponsorship/.

TRC (Truth and Reconciliation Commission of Canada). 2016. *A Knock on the Door: The Essential History of Residential Schools from the Truth and Reconciliation Commission of Canada*. Winnipeg: University of Manitoba Press.

Turcotte, Martin. 2015. "Volunteering and Charitable Giving in Canada." Spotlight on Canadians: Results from the General Social Survey. Statistics Canada. Report, January 30, 2015. https://www150.statcan .gc.ca/n1/en/pub/89-652-x/89-652-x2015001-eng.pdf?st=zjn6rCMQ.

UNHCR (United Nations High Commissioner for Refugees). 2015a. "Global Trends: Forced Displacement in 2015." UNHCR Global Trends 2015. https://www.unhcr.org/statistics/unhcrstats/576408cd7/unhcr-global -trends-2015.html.

———. 2015b. "Total Number of Syrian Refugees Exceeds Four Million for First Time." News release, July 9, 2015. https://www.unhcr.org/news /press/2015/7/559d67d46/unhcr-total-number-syrian-refugees-exceeds -four-million-first-time.html.

———. 2016. "Canada, UNHCR and Open Society Foundations Seek to Increase Refugee Resettlement through Private Sponsorship." News release, September 19, 2016. http://www.unhcr.org/news/press/2016 /9/57e0e2784/canadaunhcr-open-society-foundations-seek-increase -refugeeresettlement.html.

———. 2018. "UN High Commissioner for Refugees Praises Canada for 'Extraordinary Generosity.'" News release, February 26, 2018. https:// www.unhcr.ca/news/un-high-commissioner-refugees-praises-canada -extraordinary-generosity/.

———. 2019a. "Regional Summaries: Africa." UNHCR Global Appeal 2019 Update. https://reporting.unhcr.org/sites/default/files/ga2019/pdf/Chapter _Africa.pdf.

———. 2019b. *Contemporary Pathways for Admission of Refugees to Third Countries: Key Considerations*. Office of the United Nations High Commissioner for Refugees Division of International Protection (DIP), April 2019. https://www.refworld.org/docid/5cebf3fc4.html.

———. 2020. "Figures at a Glance." Last modified June 18, 2020. https://www. unhcr.org/figures-at-a-glance.html.

——. n.d. "Refugee Data Finder." Accessed September 2020. https://www.unhcr.org/refugee-statistics/download/?url=p9M8.

Verba, Sidney, Kay Lehman Schlozman, and Henry E. Brady. 1995. *Voice and Equality: Civic Volunteerism in American Politics.* Cambridge, MA: Harvard University Press.

Vézina, Mireille, and Susan Crompton. 2012. "Volunteering in Canada." *Canadian Social Trends.* Statistics Canada, April 16, 2012. Catalogue no.11-008-X:37–55.https://www150.statcan.gc.ca/n1/pub/11-008-x/2012001/article/11638-eng.pdf.

Walker, Barrington, ed. 2008. *The History of Immigration and Racism in Canada: Essential Readings.* Toronto: Canadian Scholars' Press.

——. 2018. "Immigration Policy, Colonization, and the Development of a White Canada." In *Canada and the Third World: Overlapping Histories,* edited by Karen Dubinsky, Sean Mills, and Scott Rutherford, 37–59. Toronto: University of Toronto Press.

Wallace, Rebecca. 2018. "Contextualizing the Crisis: The Framing of Syrian Refugees in Canadian Print Media." *Canadian Journal of Political Science* 15(2): 207–231.

Watson, Scott. 2007. "Manufacturing Threats: Asylum Seekers as Threats or Refugees." *Journal of International Law and International Relations* 3(1): 95–117.

Westhead, Rick. 2012. "Failed Refugee Claimants Find Sanctuary in Toronto Churches." *Toronto Star,* October 14, 2012. https://www.thestar.com/news/world/2012/10/14/failed_refugee_claimants_find_sanctuary_in_toronto_churches.html.

Whitaker, Reginald. 1987. *Double Standard: The Secret History of Canadian Immigration Policy.* Toronto: Lester & Orpen Dennys.

Wilkins-Laflamme, Sarah. 2015. "How Unreligious Are the Religious 'Nones'? Religious Dynamics of the Unaffiliated in Canada." *The Canadian Journal of Sociology / Cahiers Canadiens de Sociologie* 40(4): 477–500.

Wilson, John. 2012. "Volunteerism Research: A Review Essay." *Nonprofit and Voluntary Sector Quarterly* 41(2): 176–212. https://doi.org/10.1177/0899764011434558.

Woo, Andrea, and Wendy Stueck. 2015. "Privately Sponsored Refugees Fare Better in the Short Term, Research Says." *Globe and Mail,* December 1, 2015. https://www.theglobeandmail.com/news/british-columbia/privately-sponsored-refugeesfarebetter-in-the-short-term-research-says/article27543752/.

WUSC (World University Service of Canada). n.d. "Mission and Values." Accessed November 2020. https://wusc.ca/about/.

Young, Julie. 2013. "Seeking Sanctuary in a Border City: Sanctuary Movement(s) Across the Canada-US border." In *Sanctuary Practices in International Perspectives: Migration, Citizenship and Social Movements,* edited by Randy Lippert and Sean Rehaag, 232–244. Abingdon: Routledge.

Politics and Public Policy

Series Editor: Geneviève Tellier

There has been a resurgence of the study of politics, inspired by debates on globalization, renewed citizen engagement and demands, and transformations of the welfare state. In this context, the study of political regimes, ideas, and processes, as well as that of public policy contribute to refreshing our understanding of the evolution of contemporary societies. Public policy is at the heart of political and state actions. It defines the course and the objectives adopted by governments and steering citizen initiatives and collective actions. Political analysis is increasingly complex and dynamic, embracing more diverse political, social, economic, cultural, and identity-related phenomena. The *Politics and Public Policy* series is an ideal forum in which to present titles that promote an exploration of these questions in Canada and around the world.

Recent titles in the *Politics and Public Policy* series

Victor Konrad and Melissa Kelly, eds., *Borders, Culture, and Globalization: A Canadian Perspective*, 2021.

Stéphanie Collin, *Lumière sur la réforme en santé au Nouveau-Brunswick*, 2021.

Diane Saint-Pierre and Monica Gattinger, eds., *Cultural Policy: Origins, Evolution, and Implementation in Canada's Provinces and Territories*, 2021.

Julien Landry, *Les* think tanks *et le discours expert sur les politiques publiques au Canada (1890-2015)*, 2020.

Sarah Todd and Sébastien Savard, eds., *Canadian Perspectives on Community Development*, 2020.

Simon Dalby, *Anthropocene Geopolitics: Globalization, Security, Sustainability*, 2020.

Frances Widdowson, *Separate but Unequal: How Parallelist Ideology Conceals Indigenous Dependency*, 2019.

Helaina Gaspard, *Canada's Official Languages: Policy Versus Work Practice in the Federal Public Service*, 2019.

Marie Drolet, Pier Bouchard, and Jacinthe Savard, eds., *Accessibility and Active Offer: Health Care and Social Services in Linguistic Minority Communities*, 2017.

John Hilliker, *Le ministère des Affaires extérieures du Canada Volume I : les années de formation, 1909-1946*, 2017.

Monika Jezak, ed., *Language Is the Key: The Canadian Language Benchmarks Model*, 2017.

For a complete list of the University of Ottawa Press titles, visit:
www.press.uOttawa.ca

www.ingramcontent.com/pod-product-compliance
Lightning Source LLC
Chambersburg PA
CBHW071008140426

42814CB00004BA/164